神伝基本

SHINDEN KIHON

Unarmed fighting basic techniques of the Ninja and Samurai

この本を感謝のしるしとして、初見良昭宗家に謹呈いたします。
I dedicate this book to my teacher Soke Masaaki Hatsumi to thank him for everything he teaches us, and to all my students for helping me in the realization of the photos in this book and the professional photographer Giusi Lorelli for its beautiful photos.

Title | SHINDEN KIHON: Unarmed fighting basic techniques of Ninja and Samurai.
Author | Luca Lanaro
ISBN | 978-88-93322-52-2

Youcanprint Self-Publishing
Via Roma, 73 - 73039 Tricase (LE) - Italy
www.youcanprint.it
info@youcanprint.it
Facebook: facebook.com/youcanprint.it
Twitter: twitter.com/youcanprintit

Printed in the month of January 2016

INDEX

Foreword

The title Shinden Kihon 神伝基本 in Japanese language means "divine transmission of the basis" this title is taken from one of the names of the technical program of the Bujinkan Dojo, known more commonly as Tenchijin Ryaku no Maki, this book is not to be just a technical program or a manual, but rather to show the path of the technical program as one can find the true meaning of the basic technique or Kihon 基本 in Japanese, this is because without correct basics you can't really improve oneself skills. The details in the basics training is crucial to get the understanding of the dynamics of actual combat. It is very important though that you do not try absolutely none of these techniques without the supervision of a Bujinkan Dojo teacher!

This book is not just for practitioners of Bujinkan Dojo, but it can also be useful for any practitioner of any martial arts, combat sports and martial arts fans, and are interested the in real combat and to the fans of the traditional Japanese martial arts too.

It should be noted that in Japan it is usual in traditional martial arts explain through the concepts of the martial arts with puns made with the different ways of reading the characters with the same sound but different meaning, for example, you could use Kihon 奇本 with this ideogram to highlight how the base can be mysterious and will can be deception Kyojitsu 虚実, but if you write Kihon 起本 with this Kanji it underlines how the origin of the technique itself. By training in Japan with the Grand Master Masaaki Hatsumi I could see that the foundations were not only in Kata, but also consist of those movements or in those little details sometimes difficult to see that make the difference between the effectiveness of the technique and its total ineffectiveness, and this is extremely important for those who want to learn the real fight. It is usually thought that the traditional Japanese martial arts are linked only to the rigid practice of Kata, but in reality it is not so, Kata is a vehicle of knowledge you need to convey to students the visible form of those principles underlying the technique that convey the feeling or the feeling (Kankaku 感覚 o Kanji 感じ). In traditional Japanese arts it is commonly considered that the progression of the study follow the steps of Shu-Ha-Ri, namely:

1) Shu 守 (protect the "tradition") the passive study; copying the Kata / Waza of the master and his way of doing and being;
2) Ha 破 (break) active experience; you move away, the student breaks with the form of the master, but at this point the student has his own style and struggles to free it from the influence of the master;
3) Ri 離 (detached) realization; after the student get to express the discipline preserving the essence of the technique or form, but interpreting it according to his own experience, contributing to the development of the art, which is built with the human experience one generation after another.

In Japan some schools are passed along by Makimono or Densho (scrolls or written traditions), but without having trained with a teacher who knows the feeling of the techniques that are described or how to apply it in the actual combat, it will not help, so it is not important the number of Kata which you know because the reality of actual combat resides in the "space" Kukan 空間 that is between us and the enemy, thus making it extremely important to study distance, timing and angle. As the Soke Masaaki Hatsumi says; "It is very important to protect the Dentou 伝統 tradition" to do this it should be handed down from master to apprentice, something to which the Soke cares much.

What is the Budo Taijutsu of Soke Masaaki Hatsumi?

Budo Taijutsu 武道体術 literally means "the martial art of the body skill", the word Taijutsu 体術 in Japanese is used to define the ancient martial arts, unlike words such as Judo, Kendo Kyudo minted around between 1800 and 1900, along with the same martial arts developed for sports purposes.

In the Bujinkan Dojo we studies nine ancient schools, of which the Grand Master Masaaki Hatsumi is the legitimate successor:

34th	Soke	Togakure Ryu Ninpo Taijutsu	戸隱流忍法体術
28th	Soke	Gyokko Ryu Koshijutsu	玉虎流骨指術
28th	Soke	Kukishin Ryu Happo Bikenjutsu	九鬼神流八法秘劍術
26th	Soke	Shinden Fudo Ryu Dakentaijutsu	神傳不動流打拳体術
18th	Soke	Koto Ryu Koppojutsu	虎倒流骨法術
18th	Soke	Gikan Ryu Koppojutsu	義鑑流骨法術
17th	Soke	Takagi Yoshin Ryu Jutaijutsu	高木揚心流柔体術
14th	Soke	Kumogakure Ryu Ninpo Taijutsu	雲隱流忍法体術
15th	Soke	Gyokushin Ryu Ninpo Taijutsu	玉心流忍法體術

some of those schools are born in the 1100 and most of it are listed in the Bugei Ryuha Daijiten (武芸流派大事典), it mentions the ancient Japanese schools before the Meiji era (from 23 October 1868 to 30 July 1912).

The study of the nine schools involves the study of the style of unarmed combat, with traditional weapons and philosophy of each of them, which leads the practitioner to personal growth, leading to the Goshinjutsu, the physical, mental and spiritual defense.

The study of unarmed combat includes the practice of falls, throws, joint locks, levers and how to strike vital points, in the study of traditional weapons we practice the sword (Katana, Tachi, Kodachi and Ken) stick (rokushaku Bo, Hambo, Jo, Shishin Bo) spear (Yari, kamayari) the Japanese halberd (Naginata, bisento, Nagamaki) the sickle with the chain (Kusari Gama, Kyogetsu Shoge) the throwing blades (Shuriken, Teppan, Boshuriken) the fan (Tessen) and others like Kabutowari and Jutte etc., the set of all these arts or Jutsu 術 were collectively called Bugei Juhappan 武芸十八般 (18 arts of war) which added to other 18 field Ninja training (Ninja Juhakkei 忍者十八計) form the Ninpo Sanjurokkei 忍法三十六計 (36 arts Ninja).

The study of philosophy involves the study of some philosophical principles that are found in Taoism, Shinto and Buddhism, and some of them are also common in Christianity, such as the respect for human life.

The spiritual study is transmitted from teacher to the student from "heart to heart" Isshin Denshin 以心伝心, but the most important thing is to form a good human being respectful of human life, who knows how to move in the scheme of totality, facing adversity with serenity, patience and perseverance that is "the essence of perseverance" 忍辱 精神.

The Soke Masaaki Hatsumi

"Soke 宗家" is a Japanese word that in martial arts is used to designate whom is the legitimate that inherited the martial traditions of ancient Ryu-Ha 流派 (traditional schools), the Ph. Masaaki Hatsumi is Soke of nine ancient traditional Japanese schools, and he is the founder and Grand Master of the Bujinkan Dojo (Dojo of the God of War). The Ph. Masaaki Hatsumi was born in Japan in Chiba Prefecture on December 2, 1931, and was graduated from Meiji University where he studied medicine, and traditional theater, various arts, painting and Japanese culture.

He has written more than twenty books in Japanese and English of Ninjutsu, Budo (Japanese Martial Arts) and poetry, and has made numerous videos on the Ninja traditions. He also took part in the making of many movies, history documentaries, television programs, as well as a consultant on the fight scenes of famous movies such as 007 "You Only Live Twice".

His paintings have been exhibited at the Guggenheim in New York, and has also received awards from the British prime minister Margaret Thatcher, Prince Charles, from King Juan Carlos of Spain, President Bill Clinton and many other leading international for his advice as a strategist in the fighting techniques and also in the methods of national defense in their respective countries where these characters represent the highest levels of command. Dr. Hatsumi began studying martial arts at the age of seven and soon reached the rank of instructor of Judo, Kendo, Karate and Aikido.

After the war, he was invited to teach Judo at a US military base, where he realized that the strength of his Americans opponents could prevail over the technique that he learned in many years of training.

Hatsumi then began to ask himself if martial arts would consist only of strength and physical ability and if the technique couldn't overcome the strength of his opponents.

He studied with a Master of Kobudo, and few years of training with him, he demonstrated his skills having learned everything that he could know on Kobudo; that Kobudo Sensei spoke to Hatsumi of Takamatsu Toshitsugu.

During the first trainings with the Grandmaster Takamatsu, Hatsumi could not understand how it was possible that Takamatsu Sensei could make four or five Gyaku 逆 (joint lock) at the same time; nor he had ever experienced such a strange feeling of helplessness in front of that "little man", who at any time could end his life. The pain that ran through all his limbs, during that period of training, came to shake his deepest soul, and gave birth in him to desire to know all the secrets of this discipline.

For fifteen years Hatsumi worked during the week in his clinic as a chiropractor and every weekend he went to training, at thirteen hundred kilometers away to receive the teachings directly from the Great Master of extreme dexterity and great fame in the world of the Japanese martial arts and Soke of nine schools of ancient martial arts, it was through Takamatsu that Hatsumi learned the art of Taijutsu, which is the method of fighting based on natural body movement. Before the death of Grand Master Toshitsugu, 2 April 1972, Masaaki, despite his young age, became his successor and inherited the ancient Ninja traditions.

Today the Soke founder of the Bujinkan Dojo, teach at the Budokan in Tokyo and at the Honbu Dojo in Noda-shi, where students from all over the world come to practice this art so complete, the "Budo Taijutsu".

According to Hatsumi this discipline is rich in essential issues for the achievement of a high level of self-defense, self-balance and respect for human values, that allows us to be in harmony with others and with nature around us. This discipline is a way that everyone can do, without distinction of any sort, since it is the same martial art to adapt to the individual, and not the individual that has to adapt to it "is the martial art of the human being."

The experience that Soke Hatsumi has accumulated in his years of life led him to be regarded as the last true master of Ninjutsu of our times. A man of great charisma and personality, was appointed personally by the Emperor as a living national treasure of Japan (given its incredible cultural knowledge of native Japanese martial arts). Soke has great communication skills that few people in the world, have thus overcoming any difficulty in transmitting its many lessons of life and wisdom. Hatsumi Sensei not only teaches combat techniques, but the true essence of the Martial Art, as something that goes beyond the practice, and becomes one with our lives.

The Grand Maester Takamatsu Toshitsugu

Takamatsu's family was originally from Matsugashima in Ise. Takamatsu's father was called Takamatsu Yasaburo and he had a match factory in the city of Kobe.

It seems that the Takamatsu family was connected to the Amatsu Temple where the family received from the hands of Fujiwara Toshihiro the scroll (Makimono 巻物), better known as Amatsu Tatara Hibun 天津蹈鞴秘文 (containing ancient knowledge more than 2000 years of medicine, martial arts, strategy and more). Takamatsu's father received the degree of master of Shugendo temple of Kumano.

The greatest wish of his father was that Toshitsugu become a military, but he realized that he hadn't the qualities for become a military, because he was very shy and insecure. So the father consulted with the uncle of Toshitsugu that was the teacher Toda Shinryuken Masamitsu, who commented that the practice of martial arts would solve these problems because they made him grow more strong. From that day on Takamatsu was sent to Dojo at the school of Shinden Fudo Ryu Jutaijutsu that was of his uncle, Toda Shinryuken Masamitsu was a famous martial artist who taught at the military academy in Nakano.

In the ancient times it was usual that the students would take new students to try the techinques, but on this occasion, Takamatsu was taken and trained directly under the Master, his uncle Toda Sensei (Takamatsu Sensei remembering that time, commented that "seemed to be a lamb sent to the slaughter").

After about a year of this training he began to learn his first techniques. At 13 Takamatsu received the Menkyo Kaiden 免許皆伝 (the certificate of complete knowledge of traditional martial art) in the school of Shinden Fudo Ryu. The teacher giving this certificate to a students so young, was not usual, because it was necessary to achieve a high level of skill, to have the Master recognize the student is ready for it. After this school, his uncle taught him Koto Ryu, Togakure Ryu, Kumogakure Ryu, Gyokko Ryu and Gyokushin Ryu.

In the 1900 Takamatsu Sensei went to the English school and the school of Georg Bundow and the classical Chinese school in Kobe. In that time he became member of the Dojo of Takagi Yoshin Ryu school, where Mizuta Yoshitaro Tadafusa was the 15th Soke.

In the 1904 a new security chief begin to work in the factory of his father, he was a famous Martial Arts master in Japan he was Ishitani Matsutaro Takekage. The father of Takamatsu dedicated an area of the factory to use as a Dojo for Ishitani so that he could teach to Takamatsu the secrets of Kukishinden Ryu Happo Hikenjutsu, Hontai Takagi Yoshin Ryu, Gikan Ryu Koppojutsu and Shinden Muso Ryu, schools in which he was Soke.

Bujinkan Dojo Guidelines (Regulations for those Joining the Bujinkan Dojo)
First of all, only those persons who agree to this Bujinkan Dojo rules and are resolved to adhere to it will be allowed to join. Persons who think they cannot adhere to it will not be allowed to join. Accordingly,

1) Only persons who have carefully read this Bujinkan Dojo agreement and agree to it will be allowed to join.
2) Only persons who are able to show the determined consistency of true persevering self-control as martial artists will be allowed to join.
3) A physician's medical report is required. In particular, persons who are mentally unhealthy, persons addicted to drugs, and those who are mentally abnormal will not be allowed to join. The "requirement of a physician's medical report" includes, for example, persons having illnesses which risk the prevention of the pursuit of martial arts, and the kind of abnormal personalities, abnormal physical constitutions, etc. which the person cannot personally control.
4) Persons having a past criminal record will not be admitted. Additionally, persons who behave in a delinquent fashion, persons who commit crimes, and persons who cannot keep the law in Japan will also not be permitted to join.
5) Persons who do not follow the rules of the Bujinkan, who, as both students and members of society, commit shameful acts will be expelled. For example, there are many persons who, in the past, came to Japan and knocked at the gate of the Bujinkan, but were drunken brawlers, mentally abnormal, those who by their delinquent behavior put their own thoughts first and did not think about the trouble they were causing to others, those who pursued evil desires and committed acts contrary to the traditionally righteous attitude of the Bujinkan. All such people will be subject to expulsion.
6) With regard to any accidents incurred during training, either in the dojo or another location, only persons who can avoid causing trouble for the Bujinkan will be allowed to join. This is an important matter. Accidents are inseparable from the pursuit of martial arts, and persons who cannot resolve these matters themselves will absolutely not be admitted. To clarify a second time, the Bujinkan Dojo will assume absolutely no responsibility for accidents arising during the course of training, no matter what the location.
7) Persons who have joined the Bujinkan must be sure to have the membership card which is issued every year. This is to preserve the honor of Bujinkan members and, as nobility with the peace of the martial heart, to show that warriors of friendship protect the great way of the Bujinkan Dojo by gathering comrades who have the heart of the martial artist. The power of warrior virtue, the proven reason for the loyalty, filial piety and love of friends in the martial arts.
8) The tradition of the Bujinkan is something which shows the universality of nature and the life of the human race, and is that pursuit of martial arts which enlightens the natural mysteries that exist in them.

Know that the secret of taijutsu is the foundation of peace
If you study this, you can walk the path of the immovable heart

Dojo Rules (Dojo Kun 道場訓)
1. Know that perseverance is, first of all, for but a brief period of time.
2. Know that the path of man is justice.
3. Forget the heart of greed, comfort, and discrimination (reliance).
4. Consider sorrow and bitterness to be natural laws, and simply take advantage of the enlightenment of the immovable heart.
5. With a steady heart, do not stray from the path of loyalty and filial piety, aspire deeply to the ways of both literary and martial arts.

The rules of the Dojo is to keep the above 5 laws.
Signed:
Meiji 23 First Day of Spring Toda Shinryuken Masamitsu
Showa 33 A Lucky Day in March Takamatsu Toshitsugu Uou
Passed on through Hatsumi Masaaki Byakuryuu

After joining, beginning with Taijutsu,
Kyu grades Beginner
1st dan through 5th dan Heaven
6th dan through 10th dan Earth
11th dan through 15th dan Man

Ranks from 11th dan through 15th dan of the "Man" level will be divided into 5 levels: Earth, Water, Fire, Wind, and Void, and will be the highest ranks in Bujinkan Dojo Happo Biken. The 5th dan examination is of a spiritual nature and is something which is done by Soke. A 15th dan will be considered to be a true Shihan.

Currently, the Bujinkan Dojo has become worldwide in nature. Just as the Earth has time zones, taboos also exist according to each country and race. Buyu should hold each other in respect, working together as Buyu who do not commit taboos, putting the heart of the martial artist first, placing importance to the pursuit of the martial arts, and strive to become a virtuous person.
The person who cannot hold to the above will be expelled.

The Dojo

The Dojo is very different from a western Gym. The Dojo 道場 literally translates as "the place of the practice of the way", it is derived from the term for the meditation room of the Buddhist monks, a term that was once used to define the place of practice of "Martial Arts" or Budo 武道. You must think that the teaching of Budo was usually reserved to the Samurai 侍 caste, and then to those warriors Bushi 武士 who served a feudal lord Daimyo 大名. Not always it was possible to enter freely in a Dojo, often it happened that you had to sign a document binding confidentiality and where it was forbidden to train in other Dojo, or you had to first prove to have humility and patience doing the cleaning for a specific time and that could vary from person to person, and only after being admitted for training, or it was possible that the master put you to the test in other ways, for example you had to be an opponent which meant to be beaten and be thrown until you fainted, before being introduced techniques (this happened to Takamatsu Sensei).

A proverb says; "When the student is ready, the master appears," when you find a true Master (Sensei 先生), does not mean that he must accept you, this depends on the intentions that you have and your own preconceptions, if you plan to enter a dojo and learn only what you want and so not respecting your master not following his teachings, you will be disappointed because you do not understand what your master tries to teach. The teacher also may transmit only the basics, and indicate the way that you must follow by indicating how to make Henka 変化 (variants) and how they can transcend technique reaching to a higher level to Isshin Denshin 以心伝心 (transmission from heart to heart), this according to the Shuhari 守破離 (copy, change, transcend) the traditional Japanese way of teaching. In order to learn it is important to be humble and respect the teacher, once the Master had the right of life and death over his pupil, and if the student tried to test the Master, he would do it at the risk of his own life.

Even the true Master was a student, and despite being a normal person and as such subject to error as any human being, sometimes what may be his fault, it's actually a test for the student, the rest must include Kyojitsu Tenkan Hou 虚実転換法 (the alternation of true and false), what is right or wrong? What is the reality?

Entering in a Dojo where it is practiced the true Budo, you should assume that in practice there will be not only the fatique but also the pain. The pain for growth is very important, obviously overlooked special cases, you should learn to persevere and endure all kinds of mental pain, physical and spiritual, this will ensure that you will have good benefits in your life, because you will be able to go beyond your limits. The pain close the companions because you rely on them as your teacher this means that you become "Martial Friends" Buyu 武友, this friendship is different from normal friendship so that the Dojo has also connotations almost familiar with the senior student Senpai 先輩 that helps the student younger Kouhai 後輩 that respects him, the Dojo is also where you have to overcome various differences, sex, gender, skin, culture and prejudices of others, leaving the problems out of the Dojo, in doing so actually the problems are not ignored but are exceeded in a natural way, because if you do not think and so you do not discriminate, but you should not think that the Dojo there is democracy, the Master can listen to their Students, if they know when is the right time to talk.

At the end of each training the students take care of the Dojo cleaning it and putting in place the weapons and equipment, this comes from the military connotation, because if we do not take care of the weapons or the cleaning, the battlefield is going to lead to death, for sickness or for breaking the weapons and equipment.

天地人略の巻

Tenchijin Ryaku no Maki
(The scroll of the principle of Heaven, Earth and Man)

(Mitsu Tomoe)

The technical program known as Tenchijin Ryaku no Maki (the scroll of the principles of Heaven, Earth and Man), was created by Soke Masaaki Hatsumi to study the bases of the 9 schools which he inherited, in 1983 he introduced them in the book "Togakure Ryu Ninpo Taijutsu" which was published only in Japanese. In 1987, he sent it to some teachers of the Bujinkan Dojo the technical program Tenchijin Ryaku no Maki, as "Bujinkan Dojo Shinden Kihon Kata" 武神館道場神伝基本型 for the sake of spreading it, which is considered an update of the previous program, which although even the concept is the same the difference is in some parts, especially in the levels Chi and Jin, although some techniques may vary, the concept is always the same, while the Ten remains almost identical.

In Japanese Tenchijin 天地人 is the universe and the nature, that reflects the threefold division of the cosmology of Shinto and is symbolized by Mitsu Tomoe 三つ巴 which is represented by the Heaven "Ten" 天, Earth "Chi" 地 and the Man "Jin" 人.

The level of the Ten Ryaku 天略 "principles of heaven," is considered the initial stage, the training is focused mainly in the Taihenjutsu, composed by Taisabaki ("movements of the body", where you learn how to avoid and how to strike, learn how to hit with the entire body movement), Ukemi Gata (fall techniques), Shiho Tenchi Tobi (jumping in the four directions heaven and earth).

While in Chi Ryaku 地略 "the principles of the earth," the intermediate level, consist in a detailed study of Waza (joint-locks, levers, projections, counter techniques).

In the Jin Ryaku 人略 "the principles of man" is the combination of the principles of the two previous levels apply to different types of attacks using the techniques of the nine schools. These three levels have to be studied to find the naturalness in Taijutsu the natural movement of the body.

In the Bujinkan Dojo is considered very important to learn first the Taijutsu the unarmed combat and then the weapons, that is, because the movement of the body is the basis of everything and then you will be able to use the weapons as an extension of your body, is especially noticeable when you are trying to apply the same techniques of Taijutsu with weapons, if you have a good Taijutsu, this will be visible with the use of weapons, otherwise your errors will be more visible.

天略の巻

Ten Ryaku no Maki
(The scroll of the principles of Heaven)

KAMAE KATA
(Form of the postures)

Differently from other martial arts or combat sports, where usually the Kamae or position is linked to a fighting style, this does not apply for the Bujinkan Dojo, this is because the study of real combat would be fatal.

The study of Kamae is not related only to an appropriate physical posture, but is also related to a proper mental attitude, which is then expressed in a physical position according to the situation, and we must train it to be instinctive. The Kamae aren't fix but fit on oneself Taijutsu until you reach the Kamae no Mugamae 構の無構 "posture without a posture."

The Kamae can be related to three things, the body posture, the alignments, and the fortresses. And in the each Kamae, the hidden realization in them is manifested as mental and spiritual power. Usually the physical positions Tai Kamae 体構 coincide with the mental attitude Kokoro 心構 Kamae, just with the posture of a person you can understand many things about him (this is the study of Jinmon 人門 understand a person by his attitude, which is taught orally "Kuden" 口伝). There are cases in which the mental attitude is concealed by a different physical posture and in this case we speak of Kage no Kamae 影の構 or shadow posture.

Shizen no Kamae 自然の構 (Natural Posture)

Seiza no Kamae 正坐の構 (Correct seat posture)

Fudoza no Kamae 不動座の構 (Immovable seat posture)

Ichimonji no Kamae 一文字の構 (Japanese symbol of one posture)

(Gyokko Ryu's Ichimonji)   (Togakure Ryu's Ichimonji)

Doko no Kamae 怒虎の構 (Angry tiger posture)

Hicho no Kamae 飛鳥の構 (Flying bird posture)

Jumonji no Kamae 十文字の構 (Japanese symbol of ten posture)

Hira Ichimonji no Kamae 平一文字の構 (Japanese symbol of one frontal posture)

(Kukishinden Ryu's Hira Ichimonji)   (Koto Ryu's Hira Ichimonji)

Hoko no Kamae 抱圍の構 (Surrounding posture)

Kosei no Kamae 攻勢の構 (Offensive posture)

詭変の構
Ihen no Kamae

The sound of the ideogram "I" in Ihen can also be interpreted as the character "Azamuku" 欺く which means deception, in other words, to deceive the enemy through the changes "Henka" 変化.

龍豹の構
Ryuhyo no Kamae
(Draconic leopard posture)

龍豹風雪の構
Ryuhyo Fusetsu no Kamae
(Draconic leopard wind and snow posture)

体変術

TAIHENJUTSU
(Techniques of body movement)

UKEMI GATA 受身型 (Form to receive with the body)
The form of Ukemi Gata means to protect themselves from the fall "receiving with the body", it is both a defensive and attack form, by the escape or evasion, and are essential in order to protect yourself from falls and throws by opponent, this form should be trained constantly.

Zenpo Kaiten 前方廻転 (Forward roll) – Rolling using both hands Ryote 両手, one hand Katate 片手, whithout hands Mute 無手.

(Ryote)

(Katate)

Sokuho Kaiten 側方廻転 (Sideways roll) – Rolling using both hands, one hand, whithout hands.

Koho Kaiten 後方廻転 (Backward roll) – Rolling using both hands, one hand, whithout hands.

Junagare 順流 (Flowing in the opportunity) – Rolling using both hands, one hand, whithout hands.

Yokonagare 横流 (Sideways flow) – Rolling using both hands, one hand, whithout hands.

Gyakunagare 逆流 (Twist flow) – Rolling using both hands, one hand, whithout hands.

Zenpo Ukemi 前方受身 (Foward breakfall) – Using both hands, one hand, whithout hands in Suwari 座 kneeling and Tate 立て standing.

Koho Ukemi 後方受身 (Backward breakfall) – Using both hands, one hand, whithout hands.

Yoko Ukemi 横受身 (Sideways breakfall) – Using one hand and whithout hands.

(Gyokko Ryu's Asuka no Kamae)

Oten 模転 (Cartwheel) – Using both hands, one hand, whithout hands.

Hicho Kaiten 飛鳥廻転 (Flying bird roll) – Using both hands and whithout hands.

自然行雲流水
Shizen Gyoun Ryusui

The body movements are refined by the grace and naturalness in all actions. Power is the result of simple movement; evasion is the result of the simple positioning of the body. There should be a movement to evade naturally according to the changes without being caught by them.

You should learn the various forms of Kaiten, Nagashi, and Tobi, as the three changes of Taihenjutsu that become a single stream, "Sanpen Ichiryu" 三変一流 (three changes one flow).

空転
Kuten
(Aerial turn)

(this technique for example is a Zenpo Tenkai 前方転回)

SHIHO TEN CHI TOBI 四方天地飛

(Jumping in the four directions heaven and earth)

In the Shiho Tenchi Tobi you jump into the four or eight directions, and in the heaven and the earth, it is a technique to make large movements of the body against opponent's attacks. In the case of four or eight directions (Shiho 四方, Happo 八方) jumping to different sides, you do not jump very high, but you jump low, practicing landing quickly and as far as possible. Jumping in the sky means jump very high, you should start practicing jumps from this type of jump, you should practice diligently until you get the ability to jump lightly and dexterity to thwart or confuse the opponent, these techniques require a lot of agility.

Mae Tobi 前飛　　　　　　　(Forward jump)

Ushiro Tobi 後飛　　　　　　(Backward jump)

Migi Yoko Tobi 右側飛　　　　(Right side jump)

Hidari Yoko Tobi 左側飛　　　　(Left side jump)

Ten Tobi 天飛　　　　　　(Heaven jump)

Chi Tobi 地飛　　　　　　(Earth jump)

Sayu Yoko Nagashi Zenpo Ukemi 左右横流前方受身
("Left-right sideways flowing foward breakfall")

Yoko Aruki 横歩き (Side walk)

The side walk "Yoko Aruki" 横歩き, is also called the "crab walk" Kani Aruki 蟹歩き or even Juji Aruki 十字歩き "cross step walk". It is said in the scrolls that with the side walk, you can cover the length of five normal steps with three steps, allowing a person who normally runs 4 kilometers an hour to do 7 Km. Traveling while running in this way (with side walk running movement Yoko Bashiri 横走), a person can cover from 120 to 160 Km per day. When the practinioner was too tired it just needed to change side, so the legs rested alternately. This type of walking is excellent for getting through tight places, allowing you to look in all directions. You could easily avoid a person in the street changing the direction. This method also allows you to launch Shuriken 手裏剣 (throwing blades) while moving. In Yoko Aruki you swing your arms backward and forward using your fingers to balance.

Yoko Aruki, Yoko Kamae, Yoko Aruki. This is also known as Sanshin Aruki.

八方眼

Happogan
(Look in all directions)

Walk and look in all directions, three ninjas running performing Yoko Aruki, the first looks forward, the second looks at sides, the last one looks to the back.

Ko Ashi 小足 (Small step)

This technique is used to move silently through the shallow water, grass or dry leaves. The goal of the technique is to put the foot below the surface of the water or the leaves silently. You maintain a position with the hips low lowering the body weight on the front foot, lifting the back foot and you slide over to the place where you will move. The big toe is pointed down and to put in the ground, through the surface of the water slowly. After the bead has gone through the surface, until the foot is put into a horizontal position so that the plant can rest on the ground under the water or the leaves. The weight moves to this new front foot while the back foot leads the next step.

Nuku Ashi 抜く足 (Extracting step)

This technique allows to the Ninja to cross without being discovered, wood planks floor or straw mats floor, providing the complete control of his body weight. From a low position squatting, the balance and then the weight of the body are moved slowly towards the forward leg until that one supports the whole body. The back leg is slowly moved forward, almost touching the ankles, while the weight on the supporting leg, the edge of the foot in motion can be used as a tentacle to probe any obstacle that might be on the path. The foot is then made to rest on the ground, first with the outer edge. The weight is gently moved on this foot that can be retracted quickly if you notice any creaking floor. This groping foot becomes the new support foot while the Ninja continues to advance. With hands moving slightly as tentacles, like an octopus groping the ocean.

Saguri Aruki 探歩き (Searching walk)

In this technique you walk crouching and looking around, to sound out the ground with your hands, moving resting before the outer side edge of the foot, then place the entire plant, this technique is great for moving around in the dark.

昇天の術

Shoten no Jutsu

(The art of ascending to the heaven)

This technique can be used not only for climbing a tree or a wall, but also to run on a human body. As a method of training in the Dojo you can begin by putting a thick and sturdy board at 45° and run over it and then increase the angles of the board. Gradually it increases the slope of the board, practicing until you reach the 90°. Shoten no Jutsu (the art of ascending to the heaven) can also be written with the Kanji (ideograms) 勝転の術 meaning "the art of the victorious turning".

秘拳十六法

HIKEN JUROPPO

(Sixteen secret fist methods)

The methods for striking are called Hiken Juroppo (also called Hoken Juroppo 宝拳十六法 "Sixteen methods of precious weapons"). Those methods were used to hit the body with the Taijutsu which are considered as real weapons and how these are used, for example, in Katana, do not use only the blade "Ha" 刃 to cut, but you can use to hit the part of the blade that not cut like the "Mune" 棟 or that side of the blade "Shinogi" 鎬, or the guard "Tsuba" 鍔 and the handle "Tsuka" 柄, it is important to keep this concept in mind also when you study the weapons of the body."

1) **Kikaku Ken** 鬼角拳 / **Zu Tsuki** 頭突   ("Demon-horns fist", hitting with the head)

2) **Shuki Ken** 手起拳   (Hitting with the elbow)

28

3) **Fudo Ken** 不動拳 / **Kongo Ken** 金剛拳 (Hitting with the clenched fist)

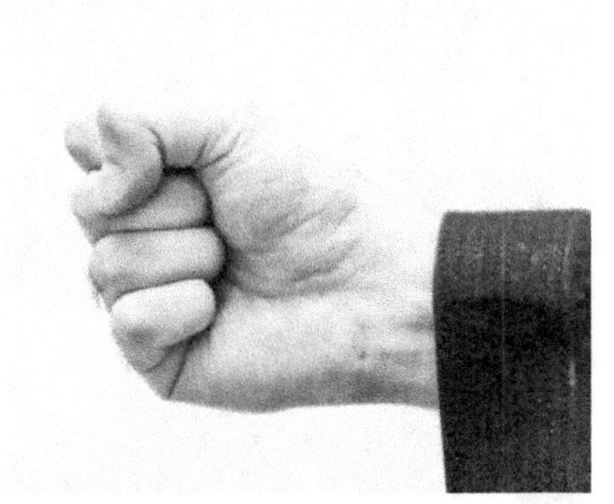

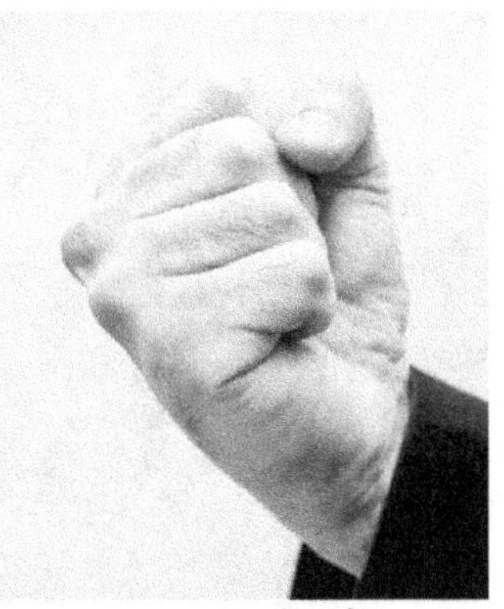

Tsuiken 捶拳
(Hammer fist)

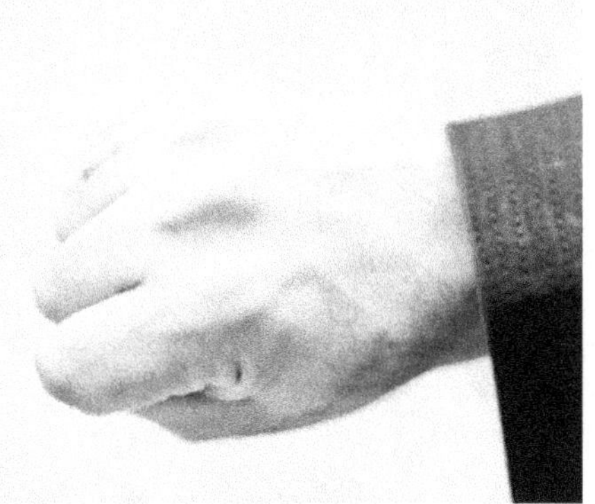

Seiken 正拳
(Hitting with the knuckles)

4) **Kiten Ken** 起転拳 / **Shuto Ken** 手刀拳 (Hitting with the hand edge)

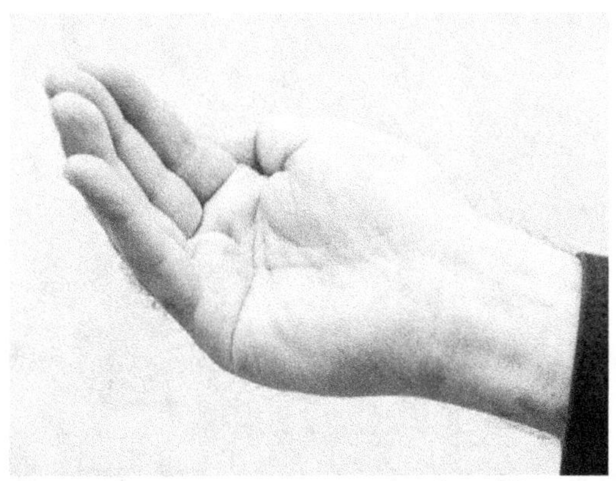

Omote Shuto Ken 表手刀拳
(Hitting with the outer hand edge)

5) **Shishin Ken** 指針拳   (Hitting with the littlefinger)

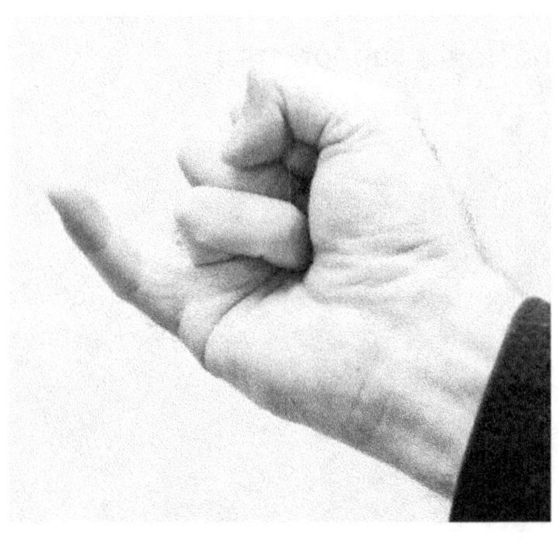

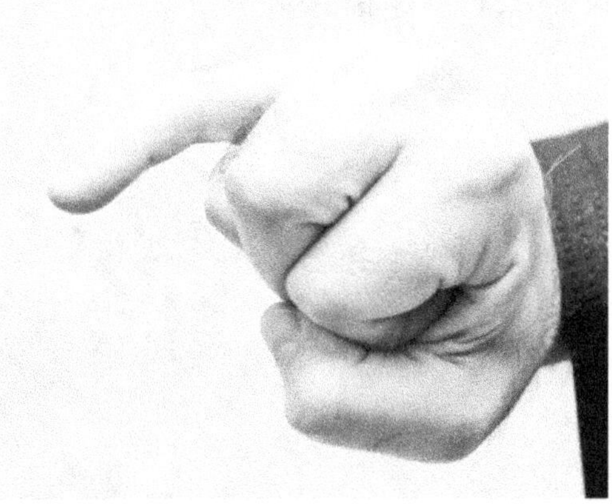

6) **Shitan Ken** 指端拳   (Hitting with the fingertips fist)
   a) Sanshitan Ken 三指支拳   (Three finger support fist)

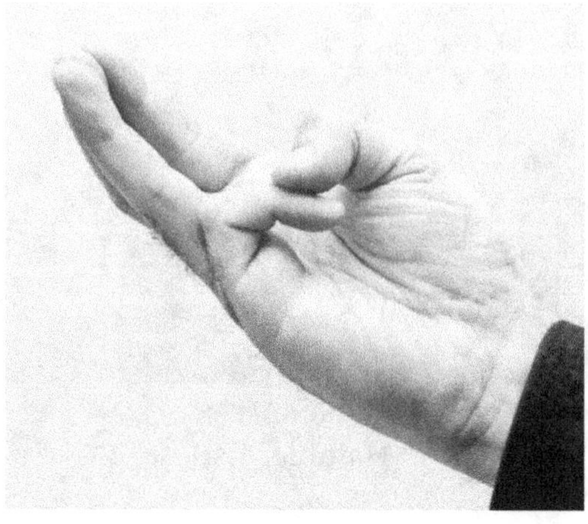

   b) Gyokakuken 仰角拳   (Three finger claw fist)

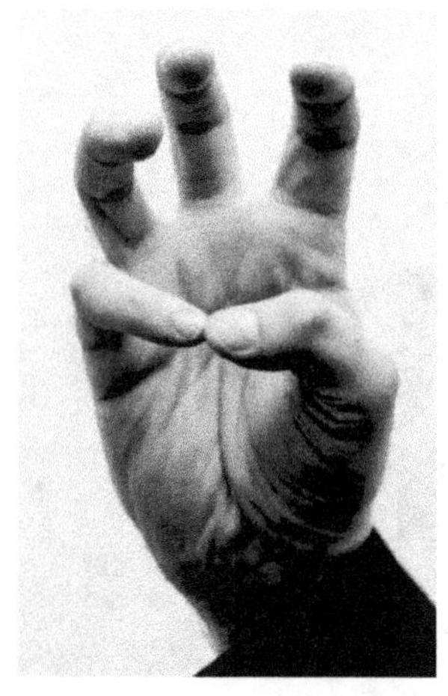

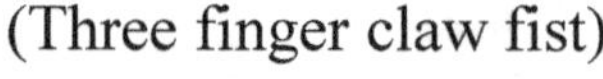

Hosen Ken 蜂先拳
(Bee sting fist)

   c) Shishitanken 四指支拳   (Four finger support fist)

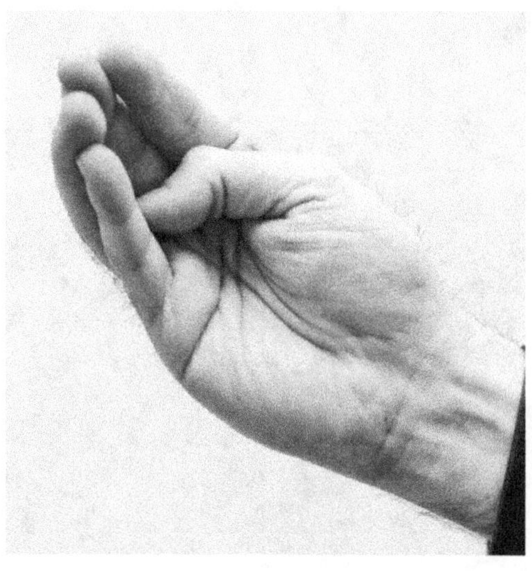

d) Shuken 嘴拳 (Beak fist)

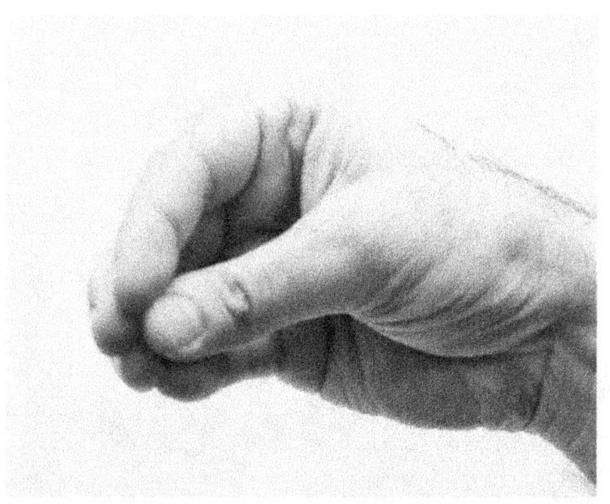

e) Sanshitanken 三指端拳 (Three fingertips fist)

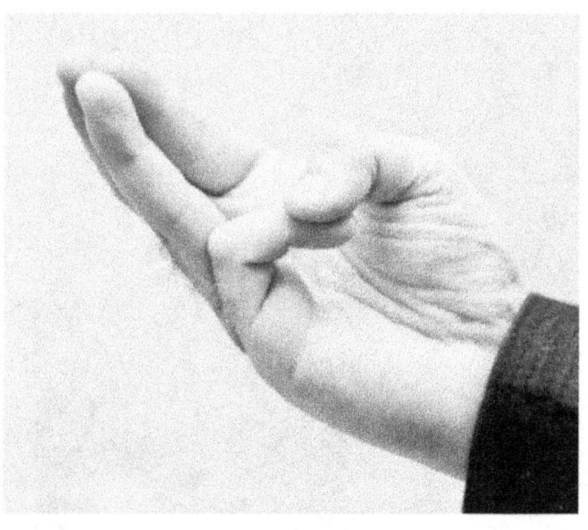

7) **Shako Ken** 蝦蛄拳 (Claw fist)

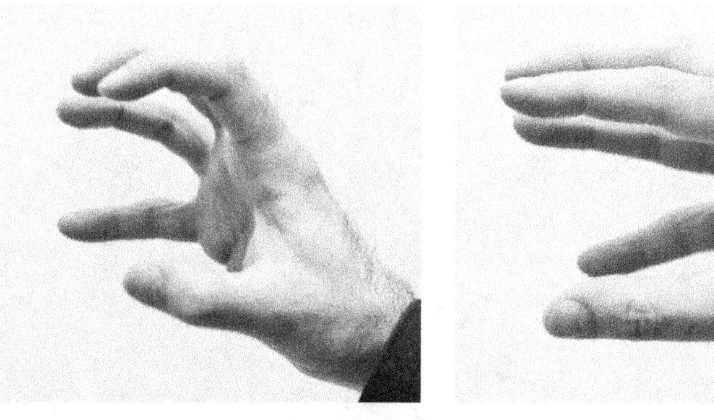

8) **Shito Ken** 指刀拳 / **Boshi Ken** 拇指拳 (Sword finger fist, Thumb fist)

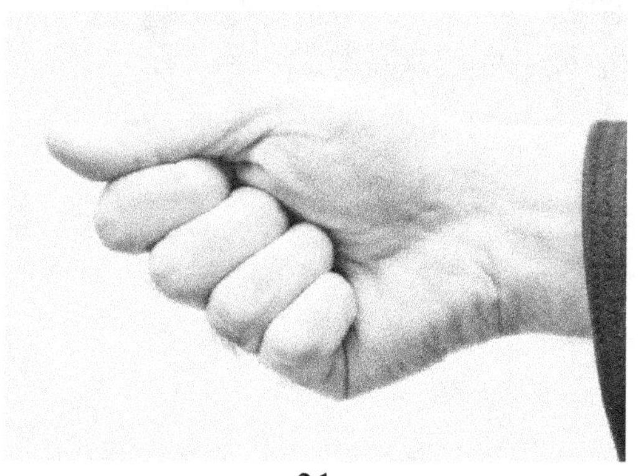

9) **Shikan Ken** 指環拳   (Hitting with the middle knuckles 1 to 4 fingers)

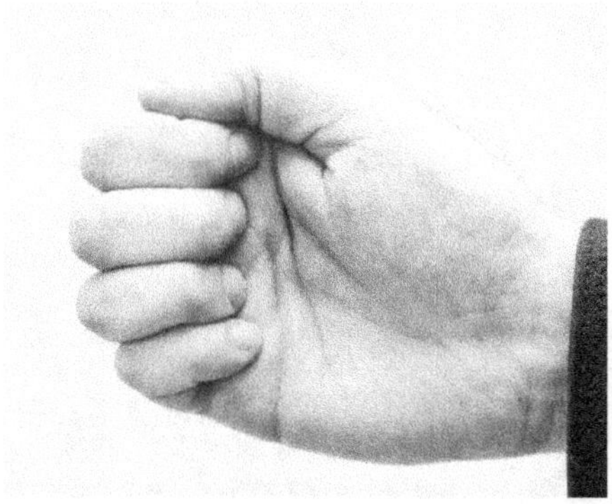 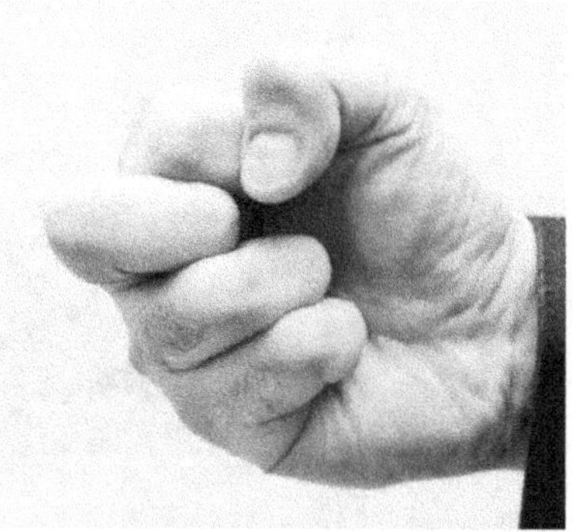 

Nakadaka Ken 中高拳
(Middle nuckle fist)

Shoken 初拳
(First nuckle fist)

10) **Koppo Ken** 骨法拳   (Thumb midle knuckle fist)

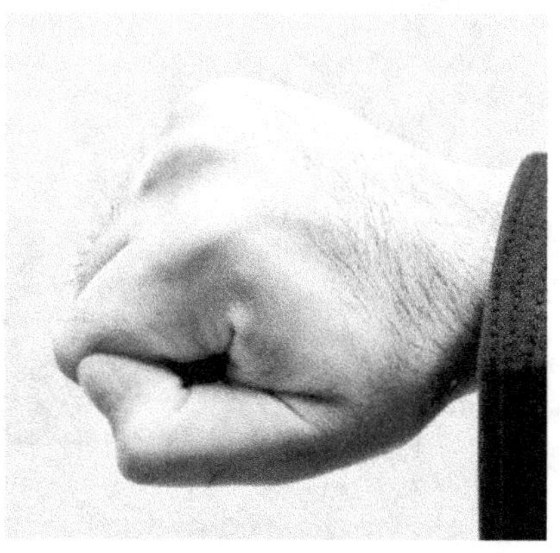

11) **Happa Ken** 八葉拳   (Eight leaf fist)

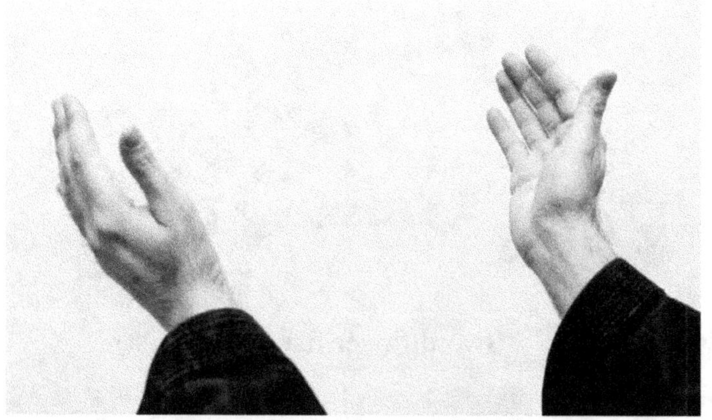
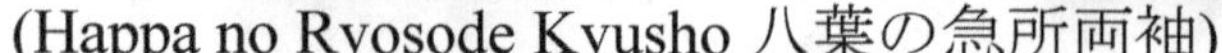
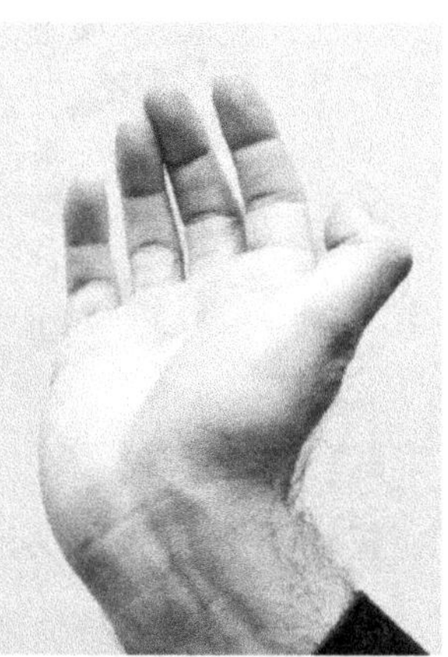

(Happa no Ryosode Kyusho 八葉の急所両袖)   (Oshuken 押手拳)

12) **Sokki Ken** 足起拳   (Foot origin fist)

13) **Sokuyaku Ken** 足躍拳   (Dancing foot fist)

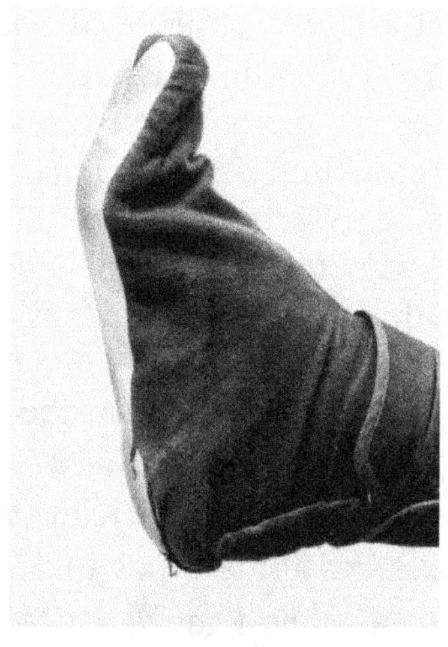

14) **Sokugyaku Ken** 足逆拳   (Foot reverse fist)

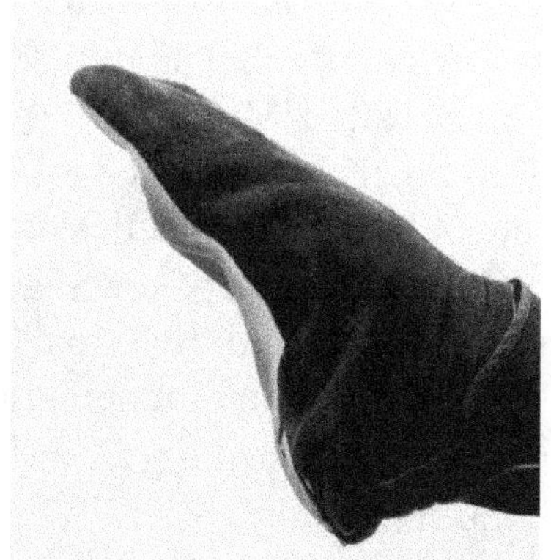

15) **Tai Ken** 体拳   (Body fist)

Kata Ken 肩拳
(Shoulder fist)

16) **Shin Ken** 心拳 / **Ki Ken** 気拳   (Spirit fist)

The Spirit fist refers to the Kiai 気合, the concept of Kiai is literally translated as "to harmonize with the dynamic strength of the universe", that means to harmonize with the total flow of energy and of what is happening around us, all things and the individual aspects are joined into a single stream. In many contemporary martial arts, the concept of Kiai was reduced, unfortunately, to the only shout that accompanies the aggressive action. There is a psychological benefit in the shout, although the true concept of Kiai goes far beyond just the shout. The energy naturally produces noise when it is released, such as the crackling of the fire as it burns wood, the rumble of thunder, the sound of an explosion or the sound of electricity when there is a short circuit, are all examples of the nature "Kiai shout". The energy generated and expelled with a strike, a kick, a throw or a cut they naturally create an air flow with the momentary tension of the body, including the throat, that produces a spontaneous roar of the real shout Kiai.

In the Densho in reference to Kiai it is reported: "When the breath is converted into Kiai, this is known as Sansei Fugen 三声不言 (three silent voices)." This suggests that you can't have coordination unless you do not mix the three types of Kiai. When the three are united in mind, it converts to intention. Sansei 三声 refers to three types of Kiai, which are: The first Kiai "Kangi Yaku 扦技扼" is the winning shout (Shousei no Kiai 勝声の気合). The cry of victory is boisterous, triumphant that celebrates the overpowering over the opponent. The second Kiai alert the opponent that you are going to attack (Kosei no Kiai 攻声の気合 also called Teppeki no Kamae 鉄壁の構 "attitude of the steel wall or fortress"). This Kiai is a shout fierce attack and explosive that causes in the opponent the momentary lapse in concentration. The third Kiai "Yaku Sohei (Johei) 挨推擎" is misleading (Kyo no Kiai 虚の気合 also called Muko Issei 猛虎一声 "tiger roar") that alert the opponent that you know what he will to do. This reaction Kiai is a heavy, intense noise that creates a sense of disappointment in the opponent because his tactics are frustrated.

There is also a silent Kiai (Fugen no Kiai 不言の気合) or Shadow Kiai (Kage no Kiai 影の気合). This is a mixture of those described before and that make the opponent fighting technique ineffective, not necessarily a voice yell, but rather an immersion of the body, mind and spirit and is used for the Toate no Jutsu 投当の術 "the art of striking from far", and the Fudo Kanashibari 不動 金縛り" bind and immobilize" (with the spirit).

当身の鍛練

Atemi no Tanren

(Fist conditioning)

Traditionally in the Koshijutsu 骨指術 schools where the strikes affect the internal organs and muscles by hitting with the tips of fingers and toes in to the weaknesses points of the body, or the schools of Koppojutsu 骨法術 using the heavier bones or the most solid part of the body as weapons and the Dakentaijutsu 打拳体術 where using the techniques to hit with the whole body, it is said that their principles are originated in China, and similarly there are conditioning techniques of the weapons of the body depending on the art that one practices:

骨指術

Koshijutsu

In the school of Gyokko Ryu a type of conditioning is to use two nuts in your hand and turn them freely clockwise and counterclockwise, making a flexible finger movement. The exercise of the fingers becomes an exercise for the whole body, in Chinese medicine the fingers are connected to the heart, kidneys, intestines, stomach and brain, and are connected with the 5 elements; Moku 木, Ka 火, Do 土, Kin 金, Sui 水 as an aspect of Goton no Jutsu 五遁の術 (the art of escape through the 5 elements).

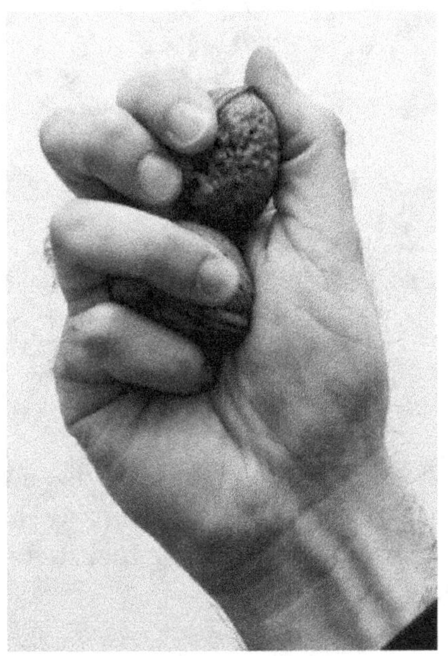

拳体一如

Kentai Ichijou

"The fist and the body are one."

The whole movement of the body and the energy is used for the strike, just by moving your body making the blow devastating, there is no need for muscle tension.

骨法術

Koppojutsu

As a method of training in strikes every day in the school of Koto Ryu Koppojutsu, was used to wrap a tree or a pillar of Dojo with straw, and after above this, you can wrap with the clothes to make it a solid target to strengthen your fists, fingers and extremities of feet. When you hit, you have to imagine that you bring the hits in several vital points "Kyusho" 急所 (literally translated as "painful points").

打拳体術

Dakentaijutsu

In the school of Shinden Fudo Ryu Dakentaijutsu the exercise are performed in the nature or using natural methods, such as doing push-ups on the fingertips or knuckles on the two upper part of punch, or practicing techniques making use of trees or rocks, for example by doing a Dojime on a tree, clutching the trunk with the legs.

真剣型体変術

SHINKEN GATA TAIHENJUTSU

(The form of the real sword of the art of the body movement)

In the ancient times, as a method of training, there was the "form of real sword", a way of training for the development of readiness to Sutemi 捨身 (sacrifice, or to put your life to risk). In this regard, you should train in the Shinken Gata Taihenjutsu applying the falls and rolls (Ukemi Kata), the form of jumping in the four directions and on the sky and earth (Shiho Tenchi Tobi Gata), then all forms of Taihenjutsu, against the "real sword" Shinken 真剣. It is very important to learn to take the correct distance from any weapon, distance, timing and angle are the three most important things for the martial arts, these techniques are also called Muto Taihenjutsu Shoshinsha Gata 無刀体変術初心者型 (form of the original intention of the body movement without the sword).

"In a cold night Takamatsu and Hatsumi went to the Kashiwabara temple, where sometimes they trained. That time Takamatsu took with him a Katana, that him disinfected with Sake and then Takamatsu told Hatsumi that he went to cut him, and Hatsumi had to grab the sword with his bare hands. Takamatsu first positioned himself in Daijodan, and then attacked Hatsumi, Hatsumi moved and grabbed the blade. The sword was old, but still cut like a razor. Soke Masaaki Hatsumi remembers of that moment when the sound of the sword was cutting the air. In another training session, Takamatsu would use a short bladed spear, and ordered Hatsumi to take once again the blade."

Hira no Kamae 平の構

The opponent draws his sword and takes Daijodan no Kamae and then cuts from top to down. Take the distance of 3 Shaku (1 Shaku 尺 is a units Japanese, about 30 cm) in front of the opponent. He remains in Shizen no Kamae until the opponent does not attack, when he cut, you pull the right foot back. At the same time, you rolls to the right, and stand up and check "Zanshin" 残心 (continued alertness; remaining on one's guard).

Ichimonji no Kamae 一文字の構

The opponent draws his sword and takes Daijodan no Kamae and cuts from top to down. When the cut arrives, you roll at a distance of about 3 Shaku from the opponent and standing up. When the opponent tries again to cut, you advance onto your knee on the left leg, and hit the Suigetsu with the right thumb.

Jumonji no Kamae 十文字の構

The opponent draws his sword and takes Daijodan no Kamae and cuts from top to down. You move your body to the left just enough, pulling the right foot back. Immediately you hits the Nagare point with Hidari Shuto Ken at right forearm of the opponent, then you hit in the neck at the point called Amado with a Migi Ura Shuto Ken.

肝

Kimo

"When you are facing an opponent armed with a sword, you need to have guts "Kimo" 肝 (courage "Dokyou" 度胸). The person who does not really have liver normally will have a false courage "Hakkyou" 肝虚, or madness "Hakkyou" 発 狂, and will eventually use alcohol and drugs."

- Masaaki Hatsumi

Ten Tobi

Yoko Nagare

Hicho Kaiten

三心の型

SANSHIN NO KATA
(The Three Heart Form)

The Sanshin no Kata also known as "Shoshin Gokei Gogyo no Kata" 初心互恵五行の型 (The form of the original mind of the reciprocity of the five elements), is divided into five forms of Gogyo 五行 (the five elements): earth, water, fire, wind and "void." You should train in this basic form until you merge the heart, technique and body (Shingitai Ichijou; 心技体一情), understanding that the Kihon is a fundamental one but it is manifested in five different forms.

As you train, you should keep in mind the mind of a three year old child, innocent and carefree so enormously without preconceptions, that in Zen Buddhism is called Shoshin no Kamae 初心の構 "the attitude of the original mind."

Chi no Kata 地の型 (The Earth form)

You start from the natural position (Shizentai 自然体), you pull the right foot back, and stretch your left hand forward and your right hand to the height of the belt forming a fist with the thumb extended, taking the position of Shoshin no Kamae. After that you strike with a step forward with Sanshitan Ken performing the movement Sanshin Tsuki 三心突 "swinging thrust" (Shin from the word Sanshin can also be written with this ideogram 振 which is the ideogram for "Furi" that mean "swing").

Shizen no Kamae   Shoshin no Kamae   Sanshin Tsuki

Sui no Kata 水の型 (The Water form)

From Shoshin no Kamae you do a Jodan Uke 上段受 turning your left arm counterclockwise and hit the Kyusho on the arm of your opponent and take Doko no Kamae and after you hit with right Omote Shuto Ken.

Shoshin no Kamae   Jodan Uke

Doko no Kamae   Omote Shuto Ken

Ka no Kata 火の型 (The Fire form)

From Shoshin no Kamae you do a Jodan Uke 上段受 turning your left arm counterclockwise and hit the Kyusho on the arm of your opponent and take Doko no Kamae and after you hit with right Ura Shuto Ken.

Shoshin no Kamae   Jodan Uke

Doko no Kamae   Ura Shuto Ken

Fu no Kata 風の型 (The Wind form)
From Shoshin no Kamae you do a Gedan Uke 下段受 turning your left arm clockwise and hit the
Kyusho on the arm of your opponent and after you hit with right Boshiken.

Shoshin no Kamae   Gedan Uke

Boshiken

Ku no Kata 空の型 (The Void form)

From Shoshin no Kamae you do a Gedan Uke 下段受 turning your left arm clockwise and hit the Kyusho on the arm of your opponent and after you raise your right hand with a swing motion doing Kyojitsu 虚実 (Deception), then you lower your hips and kick with right Sokuyaku Ken Zempo Geri.

Shoshin no Kamae   Gedan Uke

Kyojitsu - Zenpo Geri

基本八法

KIHON HAPPO
(Eight basic methods)

Kihon Happo is a basic form of the Gyokko Ryu school Koshijutsu, but the Kihon Happo is not limited to being only the basic of this school, but it is dormant within all nine schools. An easy way to understand the great value of the Kihon Happo, you just think of it as the "8" music notes. One day Takamatsu talking about the Kihon Happo said: "When I was taught the Gyokko Koshijutsu Ryu Kihon Gata, in this form of the eight basic methods, it was told to me that this Kihon Happo is the origin of all martial arts."

Koshi Sanpo No Kata 骨指三法の型
(The three methods of striking with the fingers bones form)

1. **Ichimonji no Kamae** 一文字の構

From the Ichimonji position. The opponent strike with his right fist. You perform a Jodan Uke unbalancing the opponent and taking Doko no Kamae you hit the weak point to the side of the neck called "Uko" with a Migi Omote Shuto Ken with your weight turning the column doing a circular motion with your arm to beat down the opponent.

2. **Hicho no Kamae** 飛鳥の構

Taking the correct distance from Ichimonji no Kamae, you raise the left foot with the right knee, the left hand is half open and extended, the right hand is clenched in a fist with the thumb out, located above the left arm elbow joint. When the opponent strike with a punch at your ribs, you lower the weight of the body and perform Hidari Gedan Uke unbalancing the opponent, then you hit with the left foot kicking in the opponent's Suigetsu. Half opening your right hand you hit on the right side of the neck of the opponent, hitting with the body weight with Ura Shuto Ken.

3. **Jumonji no Kamae** 十文字の構

From Jumonji position with his left hand on the outside. The opponent strikes with his right fist, you perform an Hidari Jodan Uke, then you step on the foot of your opponent and hit the right area of his ribs with the left thumb. After that you raise your hand half-open at opponent right side (this position is called Hongamae 翻構 fluttering posture). Than you performs the same movement at other side.

Hongamae

Torite Goho No Kata 捕手五法の型
(Five methods of capturing the arm form)

1. **Omote Gyaku** 表逆 (External twist)

The opponent grabs your collar with his left hand. You check the opponent's hand with your right hand (the thumb plays a key role here because in this position you can press it in a Kyusho to make him release the hand grab), you move your right foot back unbalancing the opponent, you raise the hand outside and after you twist the wrist and bring down the opponent by throwing him. To the ground you control the opponent with the joint-lock to the wrist joint.

2. **Omote Gyaku Tsuki** 表逆突 (External twist thrust)

The opponent grabs your collar with his left hand and strikes with his right hand. You receive with the left fist executing a Jodan Uke. At the same time, you grab the opponent's left wrist with your right hand turning the opponent hand outside. The important thing here is to move your body and your right hand to reduce the scope of the opponent punch. You turn the opponent wrist throwing it to the ground and after control with a joint-lock to the wrist joint.

3. **Ura Gyaku** 裏逆 (Internal twist)

The opponent grabs your collar with his right hand. You grab the opponent right wrist with your right hand, keeping your elbows down as a shield (this is very important so to be able to block a possible opponent's left fist), after you pull your left foot back, unbalancing the opponent, suddenly twist right hand inward and down doing a step with the left foot forward. Finally turning the wrist and doing a rotate step with the left foot, you bring down your opponent to the ground, and then control him with the joint-lock to the wrist joint.

4. **Musha Dori** 武者捕 (Warrior capture)

The opponent grabs your left sleeve with his right hand. You pull back with your left arm and at the same time you step backward with your left foot, unbalancing the opponent. After that you wrap the opponent arm from above with a movement not too wide, and kick under the left calf, knocking the opponent to the ground on his back. Finally, control him with the joint-lock on the shoulder joint.

(The same technique performed with the right arm)

5. **Ganseki Nage** 巖石投 (Throwing the big rock)

The opponent grabs your left sleeve with his right hand. You pull back with your left arm and at the same time you step backward with your left foot, unbalancing the opponent. After that you wrap the arm from underneath as "throwing the big rock" putting his shoulder into a lever, then you move your left leg keeping the weight on the right foot to throw the opponent by turning the spine and the body, making a lever with the shoulder on the opponent is elbow.

骨法術初傳中極意急所図

KOPPOJUTSU SHODEN CHUGOKUI KYUSHO ZU

(Diagram of the initial transmission of the Koppojutsu inner essence of the vital points)

The explanatory drawing shown here is the inner essence "Chugokui" 中極意; all these points appear in the scroll of Menkyo (license) of the internal essence, of the the Koppojutsu school, where there are the Koppo names of the vital points, regions of the body and where their effects are explained. This consists in how to hit 48 points, such as those that if you strike and if you then do not apply the appropriate resuscitation, are deadly; points of agony, if hit points that will become in the years following the base of complications in case of illness, temporarily turn off the vitality points, points that block the movement for three or seven days, those which will suspend movement temporarily, and painful points. These methods are collectively called Gomon no Kyou 五門の経 (Canon of the five gates).

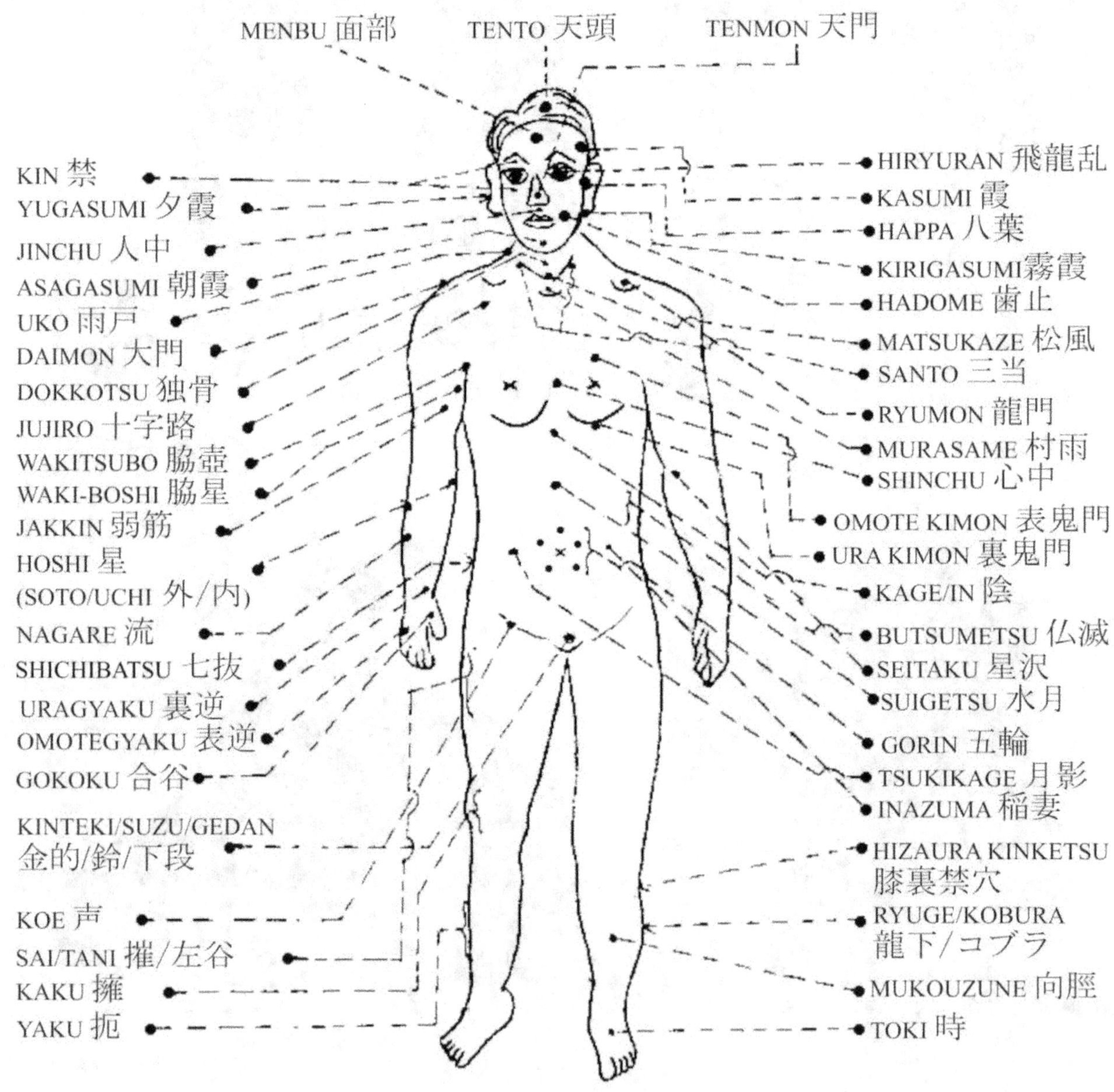

地略の巻

Chi Ryaku no Maki
(The scroll of the principle of Earth)

蹴技

KERI WAZA
(Kicking techniques)

A very important aspect in the practice of kicking you need have good flexible legs, so as a good practice technique for the kicking techniques you need to train a lot in all kinds of stretches for the legs, in the Bujinkan Dojo stretching exercises are collectively called Ryutai Undo 龍体運動 "stretching exercises of the dragon body", here are just those related to the legs, but there are also for the rest of all the body.

Ryoashi Narabe Zenkutsu 両足並べ前屈

Seiza Koukutsu 正座 後屈

Ryoashi Hiroge Zenkutsu 両足広げ前屈

58

Ryoashi Soko Awase Zenkutsu 両足底合わせ前屈

For first thing you should train in bringing your thigh against your chest. To do this, you hold the knee with both hands, and pull up to the chest. The use of the knee is an important point when practicing kicks, especially for the pushing kick, which should also put the full weight of the body appropriately lowering your hips.

- **Shiho Geri** 四方蹴 (Kicking in the four directions)

The techniques called Shiho Geri in the Bujinkan Dojo are pushing kicks in the four directions, in these techniques, when you kick you must use the full weight of your body. In the training we practice with a partner, to push him away with the kick without losing your balance remaining in the same place, you can even train by yourself against a tree learning to kick without pushing yourself but shaking the tree using your body weight and maintaining your position.

1) **Zenpo Geri** 前方蹴   (Forward kick)

2) **Migi Sokuho Geri** 右側方蹴   (Right side kick)

3) **Hidari Sokuho Geri** 左側方蹴　　　(Left side kick)

4) **Koho Geri** 後方蹴　　　　　　(Backward kick)

- **Ashi Kanetsu Kou Geri** 足関節甲蹴 (Kick with the front part of the foot, with the bone at the base of big toe).

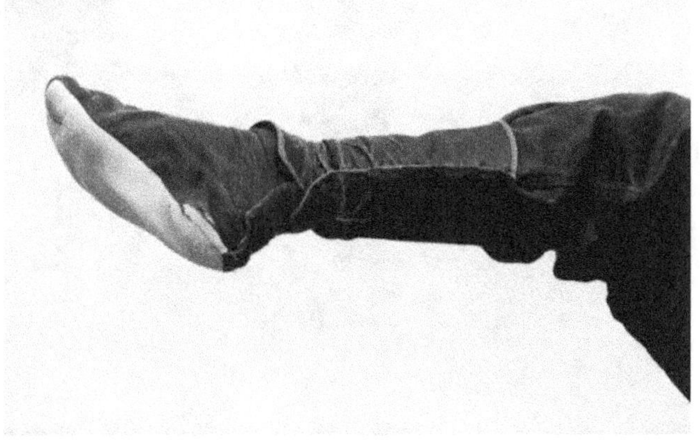

- **Sokko Mawashigeri** 足甲回し蹴 (Rotated kick with the instep).

- **Sokuyaku Naname Ushiro Keri** 足躍斜後蹴 (Diagonally backward kick).

- **Koken** 鉤拳 (Diagonally backward heel hook kick).

- **Kagi Koho Geri** 鉤後方蹴 (Backward heel hook kick, you can do it while do Zenpo Ukemi technique).

- **Uma Geri** 馬蹴 (Horse kick, a backward kick with both hands on the ground to support).

- **Sukui Geri** 掬蹴 ("Spoon kick" a kick turning the sole of the foot vertically hitting with the big toe doing a swing movement, is also called Omote Sokugyakuken 表足逆拳).

- **Sokuyaku Suihei Keri** 足躍水平蹴 (A kick with the sole of the foot in the horizontal, also called Ashisoko Ichimonji Geri 足底一文字蹴).

- **Aori Geri** 阿折蹴 (Kick in explosion or hook kick, from inside to outside with the tip of the foot, or from outside to inside hitting with the heel).

- **Sokugyaku Harai Ken** 足逆払拳 (A sweeping kick with the foot it is performed both towards the inside and outside).

- **Osae Geri** 押蹴 (Kick with the heel to the side or above the foot, step on the foot hitting the point called Toki).

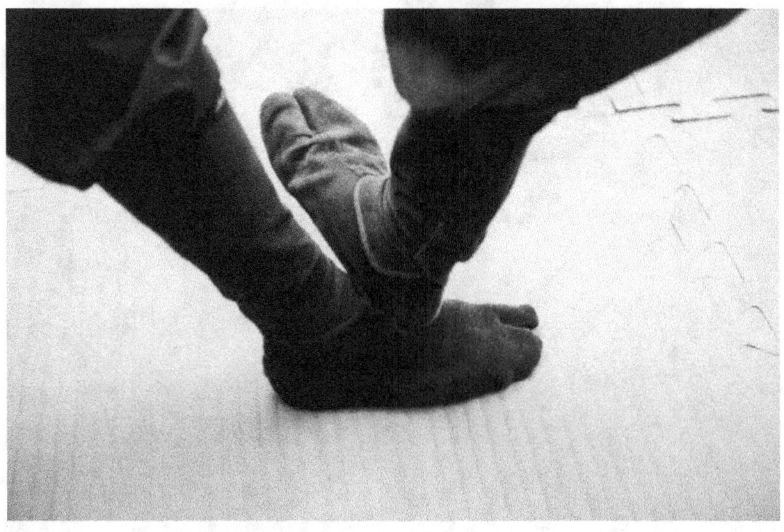

- **Yoko Take Ori Keri** 横竹折蹴 ("Side kick breaking the bamboo," strike with the sole of the foot while performing Yoko Aruki).

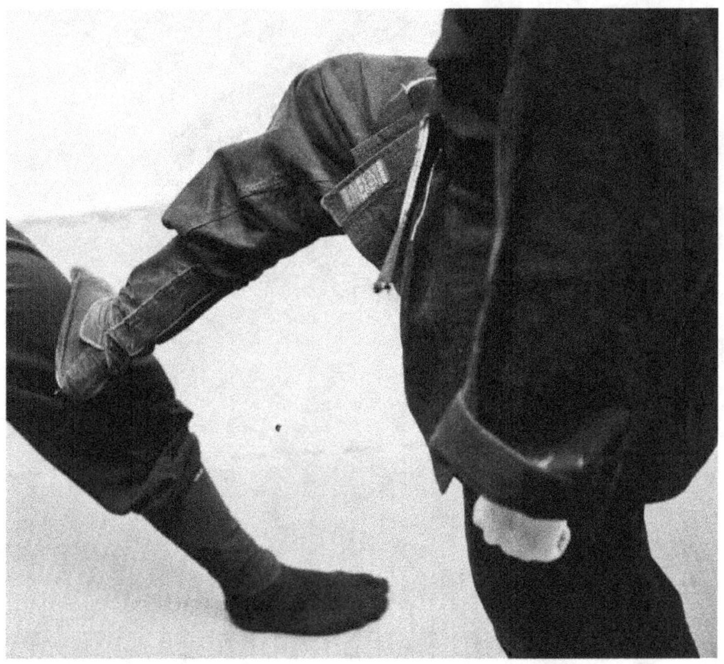

- **Kata-ashi Tobi Geri** 片足飛蹴 (Flying kick with one leg).

- **Ryoashi Tobi Geri** 両足飛蹴 (Flying kick with two legs).

- **Ryoku Geri** 両羽蹴 ("Kick of the two wings," flying kick with two legs opening your arms with double Shako Ken).

破術九法

HAJUTSU KYU HO
(Nine methods of breaking/defeating)

Hajutsu 破術 are techniques to free yourself from grabs or defense against punches and kicks even in an brutal manner, these techniques are the basis for self-defense "Goshinjutsu" 護身術. These techniques were born from the practice of Koshijutsu and Koppojutsu (which were taught together because they are complementary arts), and were developed by Ninja in the provinces of Iga and Koga. Against a strong person, it is considered important to hit the eyes, fingers and ears, and are representative of the knowledge known as Goshadori 剛者捕 (literally "capture the strong man") that are the techniques to capture an opponent much stronger than you, for this reason they are excellent techniques for women self-defense.

Tehodoki 手解き (Free the hands)

When speaking about Tehodoki, usually people think only the technical skill to break from the wrist grabs, but in reality, you must understand that the grab of the opponent is none other than a way to control him through his grab. Another very important aspect is that you don't should use the strength of arms, but instead you must use only the body movement Taisabaki 体捌き and above all the appropriate footwork Ashisabaki 足捌き.

Tehodoki Katate 手解き片手 (Free the hand from one hand grab)

Omote Kote Dori 表小手捕 (External wrist grabs)

a. Uchi Mawashi 内回し (Internal rotation)

Open your fingers and placing the palm down and parallel to the ground, while flexing your knees and after step with your left foot, move to the side, and press with your elbow against the opponent's arm while you bring back the right foot rotating the body freeing the wrist. Once released you can use the forward unbalance of the opponent to hit him with a left Ura Shuto Ken.

b. Soto Mawashi 外回し (External rotation)

Open your fingers and turning outward the hand, bend your knees while you step back with your left foot, turning your hand with the wrist cut side for freeing from the grab the opponent, at this instant you can take advantage of the opponent forward unbalancing to hit him with a right Ura Shuto Ken.

c. Yahazu Gake 矢筈掛 (Nock the arrow)
Open your hand to a fork with the index finger on the outside of the opponent's arm, bending your knees by stepping with the left foot so that you bend the elbow and you grab with the other free hand the wrist while you put the Ura Gyaku joint-lock and you grab the elbow with the hand with that you control the opponent.

Ura Kote Dori 裏小手捕 (Internal wrist grabs)

a. Hiji Kime 肘極め (Elbow lever)
With the same hand that opponent grabs the wrist you too grab the his wrist and rotate it, at the same time, placing the cutting edge of the forearm under the opponent's arm just below the elbow, pushing down the wrist so that the opponent gets up on his toes for the pain.

b. Soto Mawashi 外回し (External rotation)
You open the fingers of the hand and turning it outward, bend your knees while you step back with your right foot, turning your hand to the cut edge of the forearm to break from opponent's grab, at this time if the opponent does not leave the grab completely, you can hit suddenly with the knuckles of the left fist (Seiken) under his triceps to completely break free from the grab.

c. Itami Jime 痛み締め (Tightening pain)
Simply you rotate the grab and pressing with the thumb nail (Boshiken) in the Kyusho of the wrist, in the hand that holding the wrist, you press down causing the opponent to keel for the pain and loose his grab.

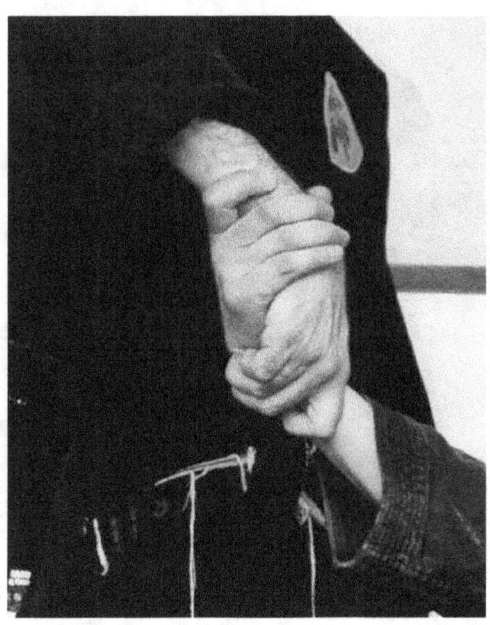

Tehodoki Ryote 手解き両手 (Free the hand from double hands grabs)

a. Soto Mawashi 外回し (External rotation)
You open the fingers of the hand and turning it outward, bend your knees while you step back with your right foot, turning your hand to the cut edge of the forearm to break from opponent's grab, the opponent's off balance in this manner leaves several vital points opened that you can hit freely to completely free from the grab, for example, you could hit with a Boshi Ken into Butsumetsu point.

b. Uchi Mawashi 内回し (Internal rotation)
Open your fingers and placing the palm down and parallel to the ground, while flexing your knees and after you step bacwards with your left foot, you move to the side, and press with your elbow against the opponent arm while you brings back the right foot rotating the body freeing the wrist. From this angle you can kick to the groin with a Sukui Geri.

c. Nakahiki 中引き (Pull from the inside)
With your left hand you grab your right hand that is held by opponent, then you pull in while bending your knees and you step forward with your right foot, you can hit the face of the opponent with the right elbow while you free your hand. The most important point in this technique is the use of the legs to free yourself without using the strength of your arms.

Ryo Kote Dori 両小手捕 (Free the wrists from both hands grabs)

a. Sayu Mawashi 左右回し (Left and right rotation)
You are doing simultaneously Uchi Mawashi and Soto Mawashi.

b. Ogami Dori 拝み捕 (Prayer grab)
You put your hands as to prayer, holding your fingers joined together, and push forward towards the opponent's throat to break his grab.

c. Shuko Uchi Atedori 手甲打ち当て捕 (Hitting the grab by hitting with the back hands)
You close your hands in to fists, suddenly do a quick motion making the opponent hit himself with his knuckles on the back or on the thumb of the other hand in order to shake off the opponent's grab.

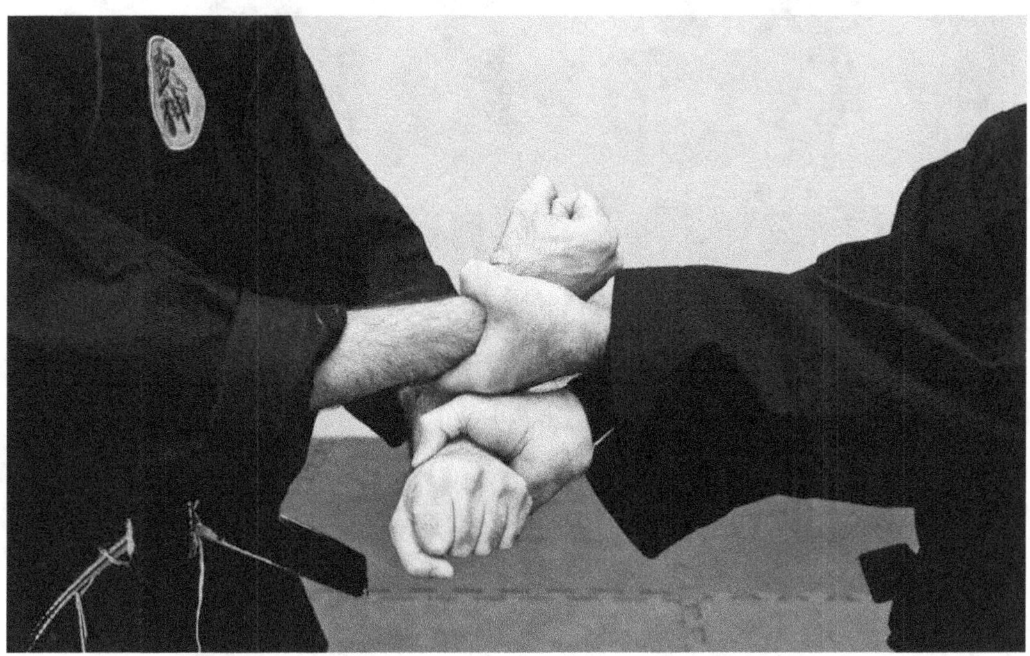

二人捕

Futari Dori

"Tehodoki against two opponents"

Taihodoki 体解き (Escape from the body grab)

Usually when the opponent grabs you the first thought is to try to escape with the strength, this makes the opponent feel our tension and blocks what you try to do, so that in actual combat this would be fatal, so you need to let go and feel the points of contact and strength through the grab of the opponent, you need to "feel" where you can get away without using strength, or by using the opponent tension against himself.

Mae kara no baai 前からの場合 (Grabs from the front)

   1) Grab from the front to the legs

If the opponent grabs your legs, you press with Shakoken or Oshuken on the opponent's neck on both sides of the neck to the base of the neck, or in the middle or on the spine.

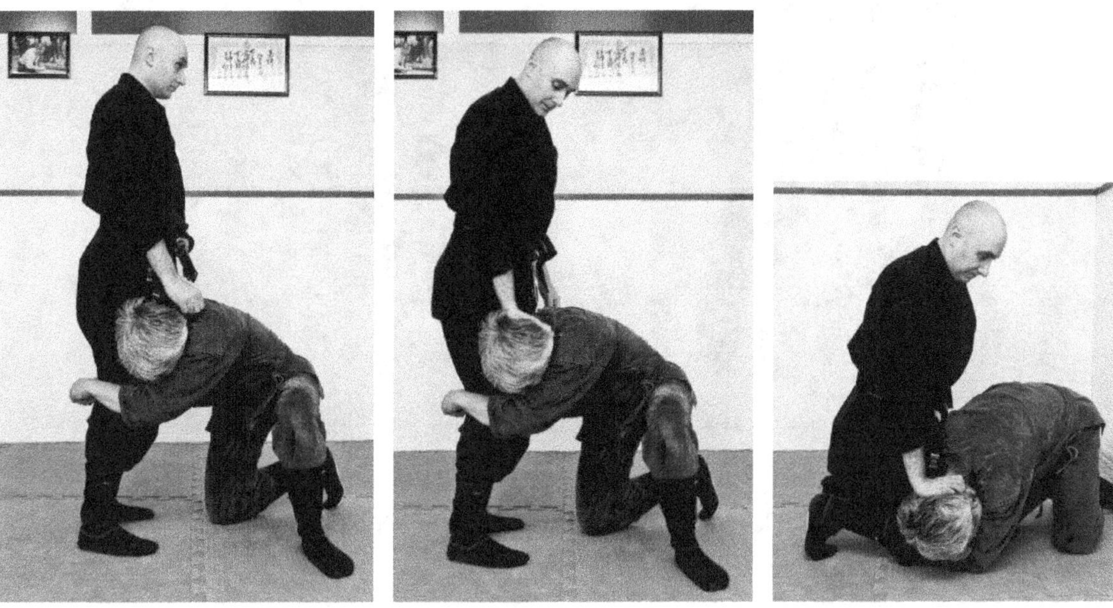

   2) Grab from the front to the trunk and arms

You hit with Boshiken on the hip in the point called Koe to unbalance the opponent backwards, and then you do a step with your right leg so that the opponent falls backward.

3) Grab from the front to the trunk

If the opponent grabs you only on the trunk, you follow his push, then you press with Shakoken in the Kyusho of the face and use your body weight to unbalance him and then you throw him to the ground.

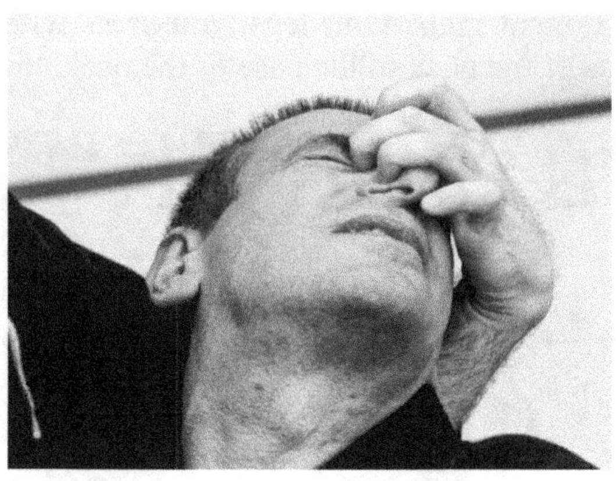

4) Grab from the front to the neck

When the opponent take your neck, you immediately strike with Koppo Ken to the ribs, or pinching the nipples, or hit with Seiken below the triceps.

Yoko kara no baai 横からの場合 (Side grabs)

   1) Grab from the side to the trunk and arms

When the opponent grabs you, shift your weight on the left side, raising the right hand with the cut of the forearm below the opponent's elbow and after you step back with the left foot and throw your opponent on his back.

   1) Grab from the side to the trunk

If the opponent grabs you only on the trunk, you apply a strong pressure with Koppo Ken on his temple, reinforcing this with the other hand. For the intense pain, the opponent will leave the grab and then you can thrown him to the ground.

1) Grab from the side to the neck

In case the enemy attacks with a Sankaku Jime from the side, anticipate him by grabbing the muscle of the arm with the hand pinching claw on him; the opponent will release immediately the grab for the pain, and then you throw him using the pinch grab on his arm.

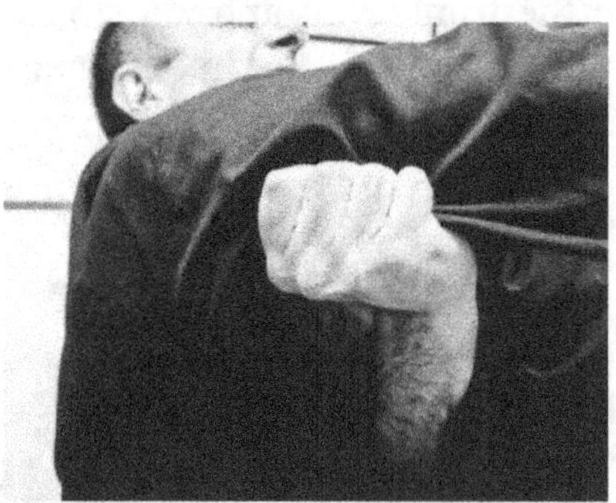

Ushiro kara no baai 後からの場合 (Backwards grabs)

   1) Kannuki Jime 閂絞 (Barrier gate tie up)

The opponent attacks with a Kannuki Jime pressing with Koppo Ken in the solar plexus, you hit your opponent with your hips and headbutt, then you rotate your shoulders and arms to break the hold and then throw him forward.

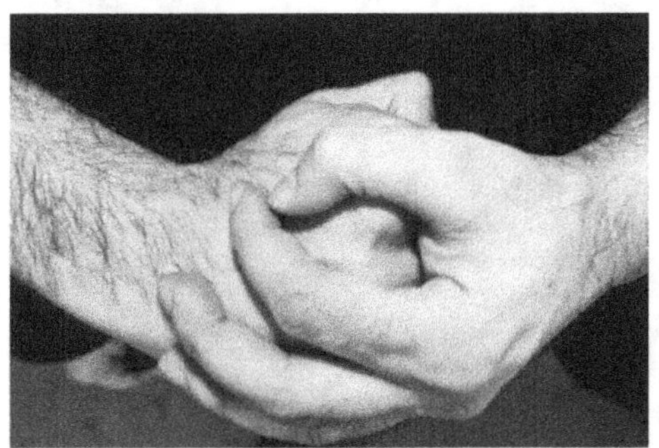

Kannuki Jime 閂絞

2) Hagai Jime 羽交絞 (Bind both arms from behind)

The opponent attacks from behind doing an Hagai Jime, trying to compress your neck, this technique can be very effective to control an opponent but it is very dangerous for the neck. From this grab you arch the spine backwards using the full weight of the body extend your neck squeezing the opponent hands and squeezing with the elbows his arms to break the grab, finally you can press in the vital points of the hands, once freed from the grab you take the opponent by the hair or ears and thrown him forward.

Hagai Jime 羽交絞

3) Grab from behind to the neck

If the opponent attacks from behind with a Sankaku Jime, pressing in the nerve point of his arm, and keeping the painful point throw him to the ground.

Osae Komi no baai 押さえ込みの場合 (Grabs from the ground)
The techniques called Osae Komi are all the techniques that are usually used to control a person on the ground via a joint-lock, lever or with the body weight, considering this, you should be able to get out of any grab without using strength, using the techniques of Koshijutsu and the movement of the entire body to exit from the grabs.

1) Osae Komi from supine
You press with Shako Ken in the vital points of the face to open the opponent's grab, and then move the leg and then conclude with a lever to the elbow.

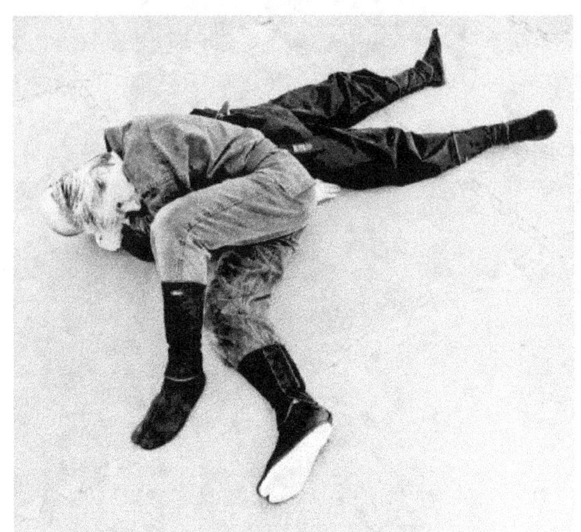

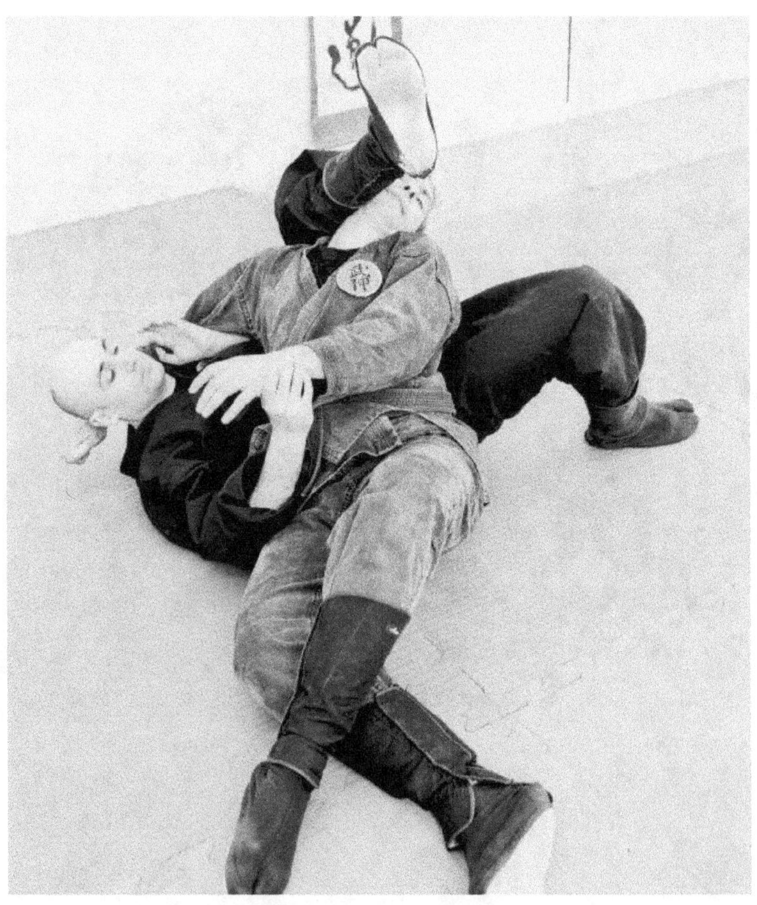

2) Osae Komi from side

You press with Onshuken on the jaw turning the opponent's head and then you hit the opponent face with the leg and put his arm in a lever, and continue to keep his neck in the lever with your leg.

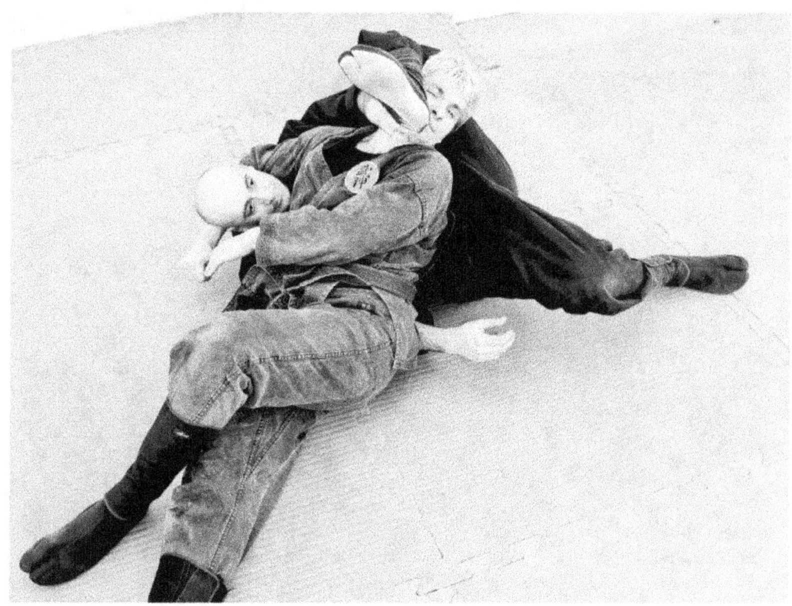

3)   Osae Komi from prone

For freeing you neck, you bite the nearest opponent's arm or you can pull his hair to throw him aside, and after you can end the technique with a Shime neck with your legs and an arm lever.

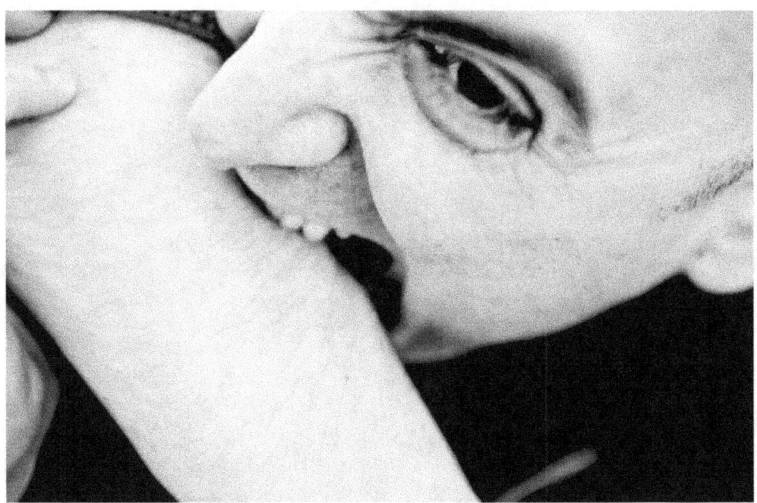

(Shiken 歯拳 To strike with tooth)

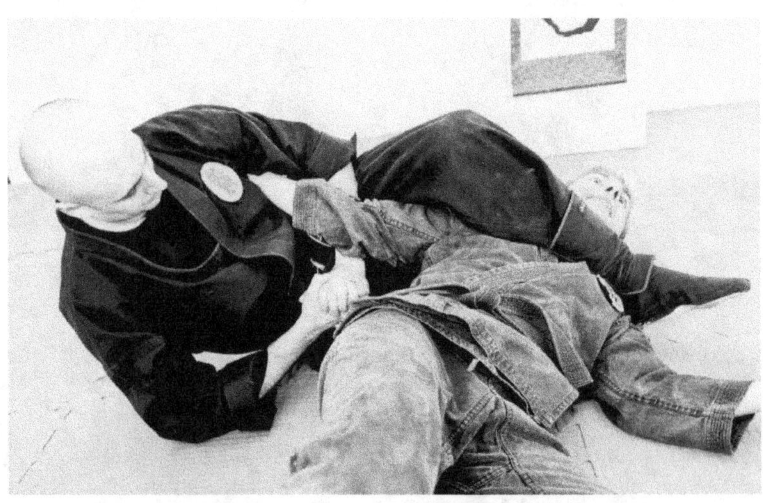

女性護身術押さ込みの場合

Josei Goshin Jutsu Osae Komi no baai
(Female defense techniques applied to an aggression onto the ground)

This technique is an example of women's self-defense onto the ground, thinking that the proportion of strength between men and women is 7 to 3, if you are a woman you can't think of defending yourself only using your strength techniques, but you must defend deceiving (Kyojitsu) or hitting the vital points Kyusho that are not protected by the muscles as the nose, genitals, fingers, eyes or pinching the muscles.

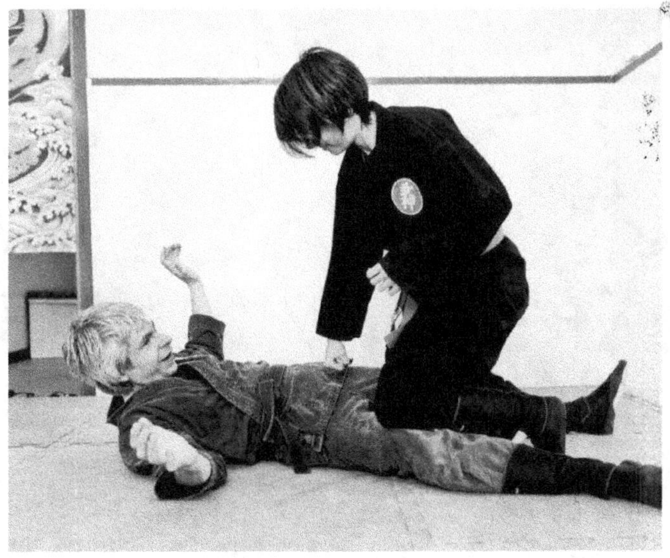

Oyagoroshi 親殺し (Kill the parent)

This is a technique to break the opponent thumb (Oyayubi 親指), to break the opponent grab you press with a fingernail through Boshiken at the base of the opponent's thumb and then doing a joint-lock on the thumb to break it.

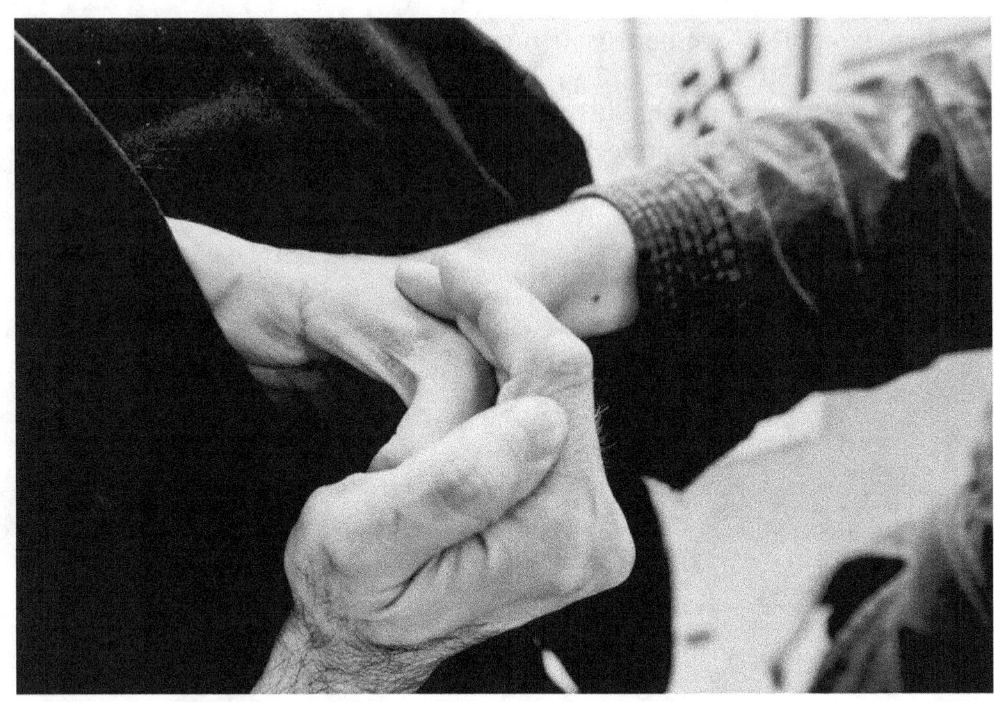

Kogoroshi 子殺し (Kill the child)

This is a technique to break the opponent's little finger (Koyubi 小指), to break the opponent grab you press with Boshiken between the knuckles of the little finger and ring finger, and then perform a joint-lock on the little finger to break it.

Koshikudaki 腰砕き (Break the hips)

These technique is to "break the hips". The opponent try to throw you, to neutralize the throw you simply lower your hips and step back, this will do break the opponent's balance and allows you to hit into the sciatic nerve on the hips vital point called Shichibatsu 七抜 (which means "not being able to get up for seven days").

   1) Shichibatsu Tsuki Ire 七抜突き入れ (Entering strike in sciatic nerve point)

When the opponent from Kumiuchi tries to throw you, you control with your hand the opponent's grab then moving sideways and using the Boshi Ken to press the point called Shichibatsu.

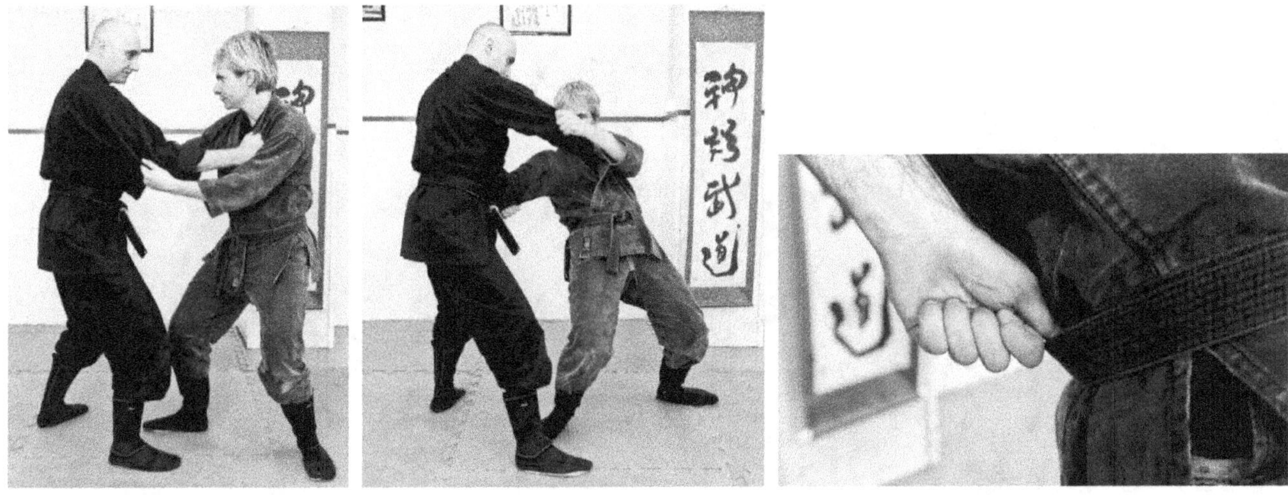

   2) Shichibatsu Kekomi 七抜蹴込み (Kick in sciatic nerve point)

When the opponent from Kumiuchi tries to throw you, you control with your hand the opponent's grab then moving sideways and kick with your heel in Shichibatsu.

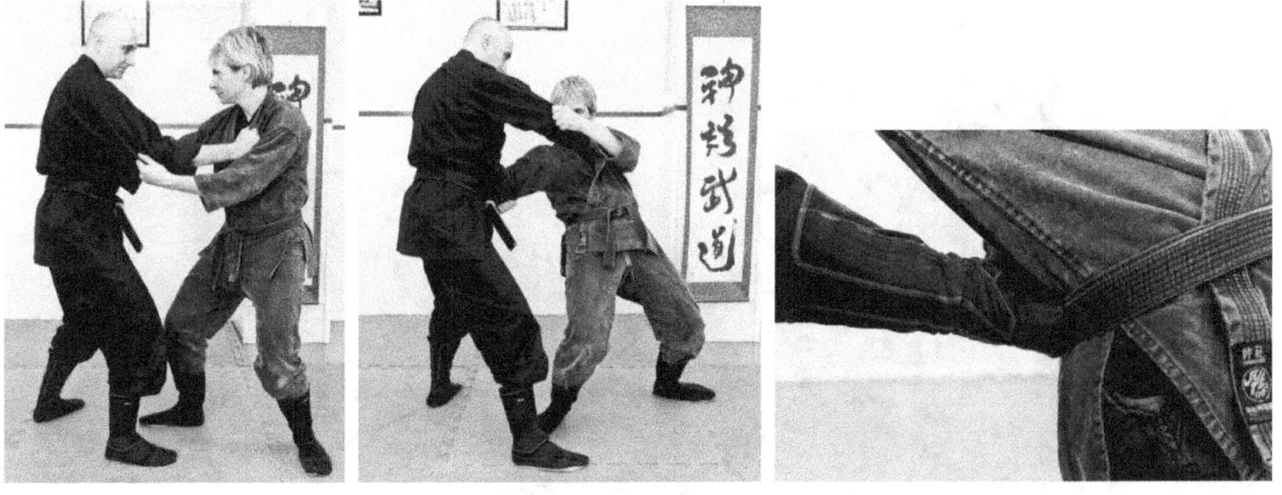

91

Happogeri 八方蹴
(Kicking in the eight directions)

This form of kicking not only includes the hit with the only purpose of hurting, but also kicks to test the reactions of the opponent while maintaining a certain distance, and examine the possibilities and find out the weak spots (this is defined as Shirabe Gata 調べ型). Happo Geri involves kicking the opponent from different angles and in infinite ways, has no fixed form, you must train kicking several vital points from different angles.

1) Sai Geri 摧蹴 (Kick to inside the thigh)

The opponent strikes with a punch, you avoid it with Yoko Aruki and kick inside the thigh of the front leg.

2) Gaisai Geri 外摧蹴 (Kick to the side of the thigh)

The opponent strikes with a punch, you avoid it with Yoko Aruki and kick the side of the thigh of the back leg with the heel.

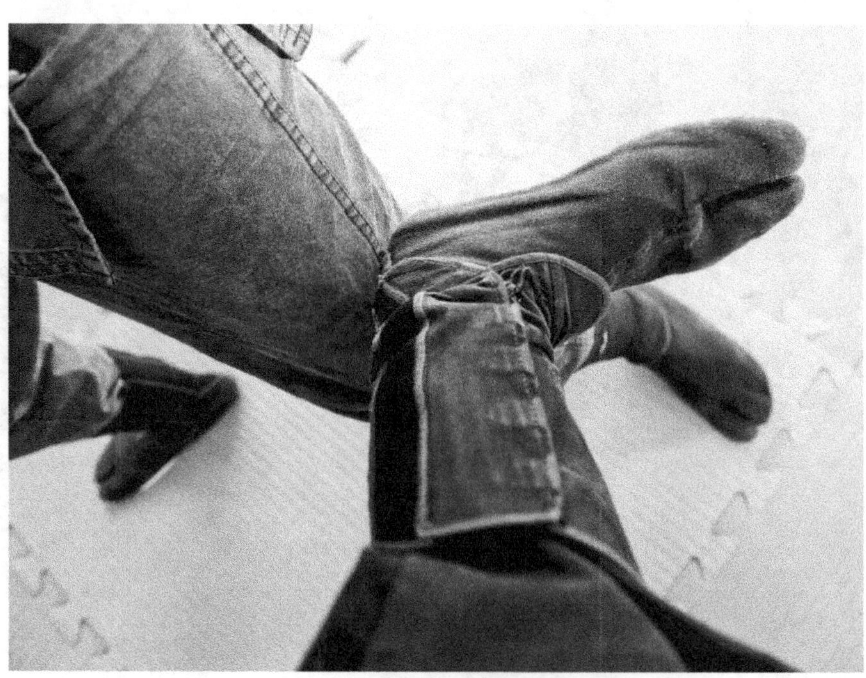

3) Kosei Geri 虚生蹴 (Kick to groin)
The opponent strikes with a punch, you avoid inside and kick to the groin with Sukui Geri.

八方蹴

Happogeri

Keri Gaeshi 蹴返し (Kicks counter techniques)

1) Keri Gaeshi Ichi 蹴返し一 (Kicks counter techniques 1)

When the opponent kicks, you avoid externally and kick the calf in the vital point called Kobura, hitting pretty strongly the opponent will fall back and when he rises he can't use that leg, so when you do this technique you must be very careful learning to control your strength when hitting.

2) Keri Gaeshi Ni 蹴返し二 (Kicks counter techniques 2)
When the opponent kicks, you avoid internally hitting with a right Fudo Ken in Naisai and quickly kick the other leg with the left Sokuyaku Ken always in the Naisai.

3) Keri Gaeshi San 蹴返し三 (Kicks counter techniques 3)
When the opponent kicks, you avoid internally doing Yoko Aruki while you protect yourself with Gedan Uke and then strike with Sokuyaku Ken to the opponent knee (in training when you do this technique you should be careful so to not break the opponent's knee).

Kerikudaki 蹴砕き (Smash kick)

1) Keri Harai 蹴払い (Sweeping kick)

When the opponent strikes with a punch, you kick the arm sweeping to aside with Sokugyaku Ken Harai (internal and external).

2) Keri Age 蹴上げ (Upward kick)

When the opponent strikes with a punch, you kick the arm upward with Ashi Kanetsu Kou Geri.

3) Keri Otoshi 蹴落し (Downward kick)

When the opponent strikes with a punch, you kick the arm down with Sokuyaku Ken.

Kenkudaki 拳砕き (Smash the fist)

1) Kenkudaki no waza Ichi 拳の技一 (Smash the fist technique 1)

When the opponent strikes with a punch, you avoid externally striking with Seiken the back of the hand, immediately follow with a Fudo Ken on the triceps muscle.

2) Kenkudaki no waza Ni 拳の技二 (Smash the fist technique 2)

When the opponent strikes with a punch, you do a Jodan Uke upward and strike with Fudo Ken inside the biceps or you can strike in the armpit with Shikan Ken.

3) Kenkudaki no waza San 拳の技三 (Smash the fist technique 3)

When the opponent's strikes with a punch, you do a Jodan Uke to the arm and strike with the other hand with an Omote Shuto Ken over his bicep.

NAGE KATA
(Throw form)

In the Taijutsu there are an infinite number of techniques that allow you to throw the opponent, but to throw the opponent you have to wait for the right moment when your opponent thinks he has won and his guard is down. It is very important to practice the throw with the movement of the body keeping your back straight, the most common mistake is to use the unnatural positions and forcing the technique, making it easy for the opponent to counter the throwing technique.

Long ago, there were evil warriors that tested their skills by practicing the "Tsujigiri" 辻斬 (testing the sword on innocent victims). Once when Takamatsu Sensei was 18, while working in the factory of his father there was need about 1250 liters of clean water for a day. Takamatsu Sensei every morning, using a pole and four brackets, took all the water to the factory. The water came from the mouth of a turtle stone, which consistently gave out clear water. This turtle was located just below the mountain Maruyama, that was a few kilometers away from the factory. Each load weighed about 240 kg and needed a total of five trips from the turtle, Takamatsu Sensei said that this was perfect to condition his legs and hips.

One day a worker talking with Takamatsu Sensei said: "Young master, I had a hell of a time last night. I was working alone on Shinbashi bridge when a man locked my way. If I moved to the right to pass him, he moved to block me and did the same if I moved to the left. Then, he grabbed me by my collar and threw me into the water. I thought I was going to be killed. Young master, I don't really want to go on errands in that area after dark." Listening this conversation, another worker joined them saying: "Really? It's happened the same to me. Doesn't this look like the Tsujigiri of ancient times?" Hearing this, Takamatsu Sensei said: "Leave it to me."

The bridge of Shinbashi is in the point where the river enters into the sea, where sailors tie their small boats to the docks and then sail to the sea. That night Takamatsu Sensei crossed the Shinbashi bridge four or five times without anything happening. The next day he did the same thing with the same result, then he thought that this criminal probably is someone who knew him, the next night he put on a disguise and went to the bridge. As expected, when he was halfway across the bridge, a man wearing a hat that covered his eyes, walked towards him. Takamatsu Sensei moved to the left to pass it, but the guy moved on his way. The same thing happened when he tried to right, he then grabbed Takamatsu by the collar trying to project him using the hips, Takamatsu moved backward the hips and let his arms lean down naturally. The man tried unsuccessfully to throw him and then he try to hit Takamatsu with a fist, and a kick. But all of his punches and kicks hit the air, when this man became confused by his unsuccessful attacks, Takamatsu Sensei throw him upside down, with a Kiai yell. The man's hat flew off and he fell on his stomach, Takamatsu Sensei turned the man to see his face and applied the art of resuscitation (Kappo 活法). It was one of the students of Mizuta Sensei (teacher of Takagi Yoshin Ryu Jutaijutsu school), which had the license of the average level in Jutaijutsu. Takamatsu Sensei angrily said: "How could you bring dishonor to your school in this way? You should be ashamed!"

組み打ち

Kumiuchi

(Grapple)

In actual combat when you're grappling with the opponent, you should not forget that each grip to the collar can be a control point, a point to cause pain and that also the opponent can use it too.

柔体術

Jutaijutsu

"The difference between Judo and Jutaijutsu is that in Judo you intend to throw someone, then you tend to use the strength and speed to try to win. This means, of course, that with age, you lose your skills. With Jutaijutsu throw, you do not have the intention to throw. It is simply trying to take advantage of the weakness of your opponent. And since these techniques do not rely on strength, your ability does not deteriorate with time, rather you will continue to improve because you will not use any strength to apply the techniques."

Soke Masaaki Hatsumi

Ganseki Nage 巌石投 (The big rock throw)

From the grappling pose called Kumiuchi, you grab the forearm of the opponent and you pull it to you, after you move your right arm under his armpit, like to throw a big rock, and continuing the movement throw the opponent with your back.

Ganseki Otoshi 巖石落 (The big rock fall)
From the grappling pose called Kumiuchi, you grab the forearm of the opponent and you pull it to you, you move your right arm under the armpit, like to throw a large rock, if the opponent drop his body making it too difficult to throw him, you use your leg to make him fall down and put pressure on his arm.

Ganseki Ori 巖石折 (The big rock break)
From the grappling pose called Kumiuchi, you grab the forearm of the opponent and you pull it to you, you move your right arm under the armpit, like to throw a large rock, if the opponent brings backwards his hips to avoid the throw, you put the leg in order to place the lever in one or both legs to throw the opponent.

Ogoshi 大腰 (Big hips)

From the grappling pose called Kumiuchi, you take a step back to unbalance the opponent and arching him forward, at this point you can easily enter with your hips moving your hand under his arm to grab the belt from the back to bee able to throw with the hips.

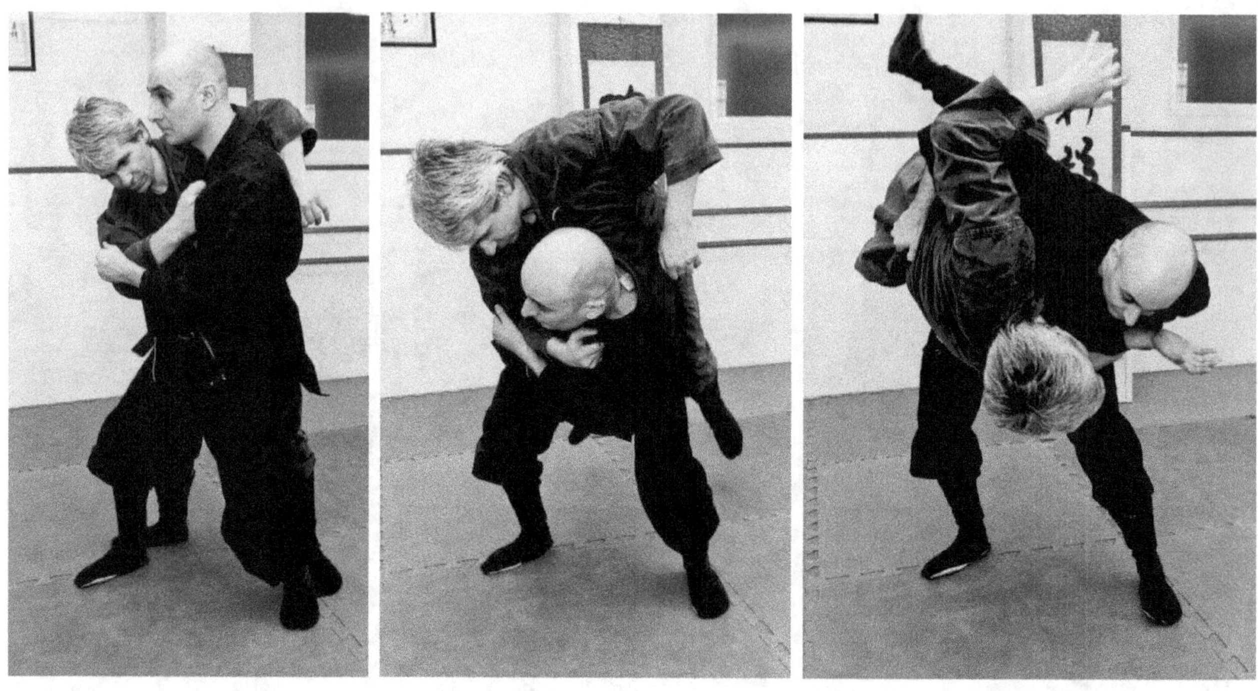

Harai Goshi 拂腰 (Sweeping hips)

From the grappling pose called Kumiuchi, you take a step back to unbalance the opponent and arching him forward, at this point you can easily enter with your hips moving your hand under his arm to grab the belt from the back, at the same time with your leg sweep the opponent's leg to throw with the hips.

Koshi Guruma 腰車 (Wheel hips)

From the grappling pose called Kumiuchi, you take a step back to unbalance the opponent and is arching him forward, at this point you can easily enter with your hips moving your hand under his arm to grab the belt from the front and from behind to can throw with the hips, turn the opponent to make him fall on the head (when you are training this technique you should be very careful when you throw your opponent without getting him hurt).

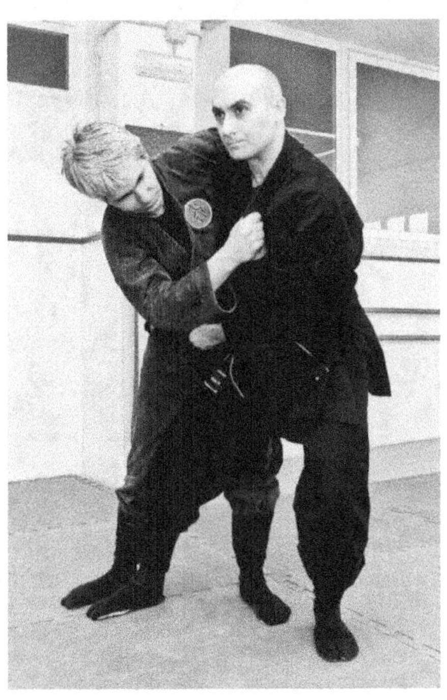

Hane Goshi 跳腰 (Wing hips)

From the grappling pose called Kumiuchi, you take a step back to unbalance the opponent, arching him forward, at this point you can easily enter with your hips moving your hand under his arm to grab the belt from the back, at the same time with your leg kick the opponent's thigh to throw with the hips.

Uchimata 内股 (Inner thigh)

From the grappling pose called Kumiuchi, you take a step back to unbalance the opponent by pressing with Boshiken in Ryumon, suddenly you turn on the leg to kick with the other leg in the Naisai and so that you can throw the opponent, in this technique the most important thing is the initial unbalance on the opponent.

Osoto 大外 (Big exterior)

From the grappling pose called Kumiuchi, you take a step back to unbalance the opponent by pressing with Boshiken in Ryumon, then you step outside and kick with a Koken's on the leg to throw him.

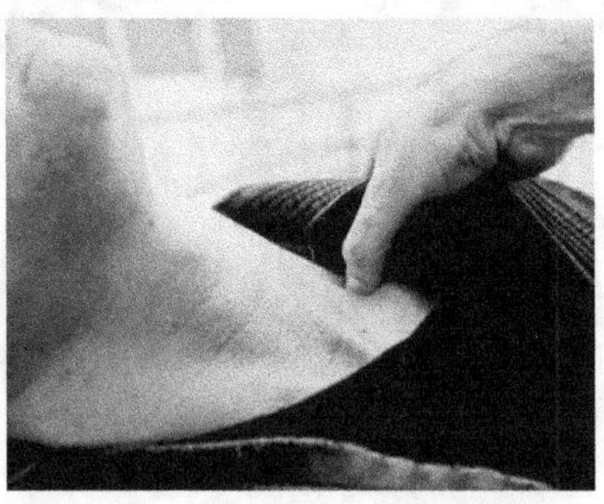

Kosoto 小外 (Small exterior)

From the grappling pose called Kumiuchi, you take a step back to unbalance the opponent by pressing with Boshiken in Ryumon, then you step outside with Yoko Aruki and sweep with the foot the opponent's leg to make him fall.

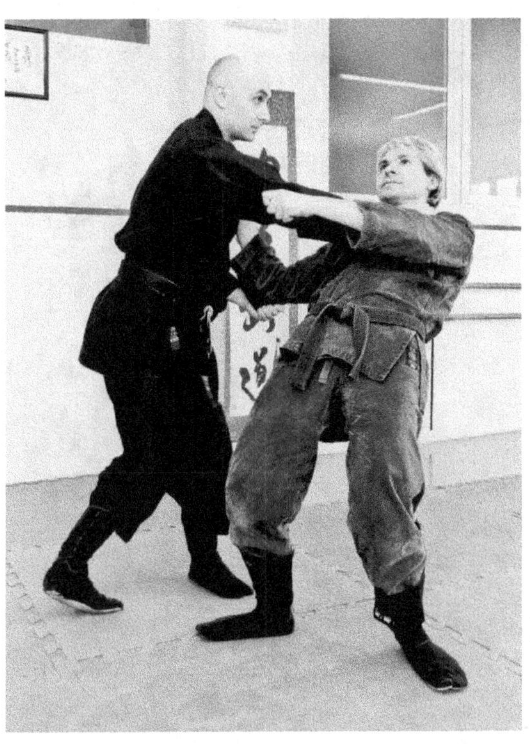

Kouchi 小内 (Small internal)

From the grappling pose called Kumiuchi, you take a step back to unbalance the opponent by pressing with Boshiken in Ryumon, then you step inside with Yoko Aruki and sweep with the foot the opponent's leg to make him fall.

Ashibarai 足払 (Leg sweep)
From the grappling pose called Kumiuchi, you take a step back to unbalance the opponent by pressing with Boshiken in Ryumon and pulling him by the collar of the sleeve to make him twist, just when he is unbalanced you sweep the leg hitting just above the ankle throwing the opponent to the ground.

足らう

Ashirau

In addition to learn to sweep with the sole of the foot you should learn to utilize the parts of the shinbone, the calf, the heel, the edge of the foot, the toe of the foot and the big toe.

Ippon Seoinage 一本背負投 (One arm back throw)

From the grappling pose called Kumiuchi, you take a step back to unbalance the opponent, you grab with the right hand the collar of the sleeve bending the opponent's arm to enter with your hips and then throw the opponent.

Morote Seoinage 諸手背負投 (Both arms back throw)

From the grappling pose called Kumiuchi, you take a step back to unbalance the opponent keeping the grab on the lapel and enter with your hips and then throw the opponent. If desired, instead of grabbing the collar you can grab the other arm.

Katate Gyaku Seoinage 片手逆背負投 (One arm joint-lock back throw)

From the grappling pose called Kumiuchi, you take a step back to unbalance the opponent, you enter from outside while twisting his wrist entering under the arm with the body by putting the arm in a lever, by raising the opponent on his tiptoes you load him with the hips and throw him.

Morote Gyaku Seoinage 諸手逆背負投 (Both arms joint-lock back throw)

From the grappling pose called Kumiuchi, you take a step back to unbalance the opponent, you enter from outside while you twist both opponent's wrists and entering under his arms with the body by putting them in a lever, by raising the opponent on his tiptoes you load with the hips and throw him.

Henka 変化 (Variation)

Itami Nage 痛投 (Painful throw)
The throw called Itami Nage "Painful throw" consist in a throw using the painful pressure points of Kyusho like Omote Kimon, Mimi, Kirigasumi, etc., or by grasping the hair.

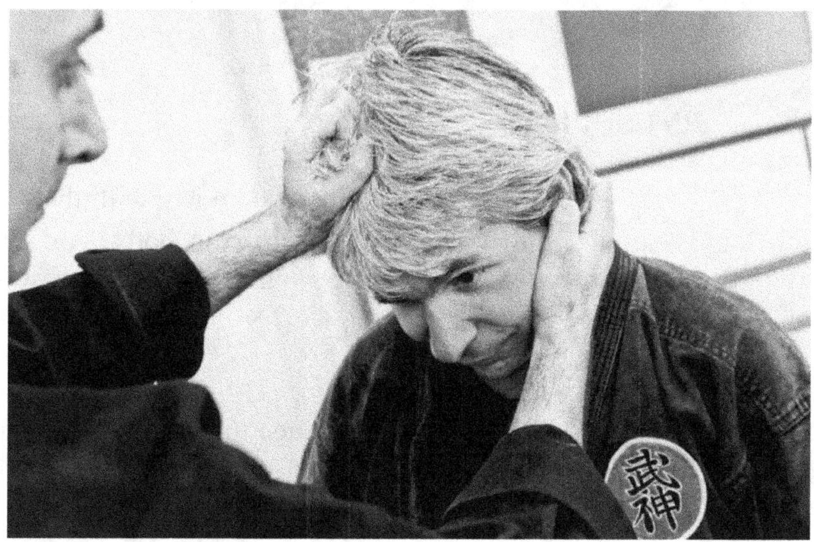 

Taki Otoshi 瀧落 (Waterfall fall)
The throw called Taki Otoshi or "Waterfall fall" is to the accompaniment of throw in letting go the opponent when is at the highest point of the throw, so it is not possible to do a proper Ukemi.
This principle can be applied to all throwing techniques, it is important in training the safety of your partner and practice it only after learning how to do a good Ukemi, a way to train is to land without injury by performing a back flip while the opponent throws you.

流水行き

RYUSUI IKI
(Follow the flow of water)

The Techniques called Ryusui Iki 流水行き "follow the water flow," are also known with the name Sutemi Nage 捨身投 "throw by sacrificing oneself", rather than throw with your body, you leave yourself to follow the flow, the strength of the opponent, sacrificing your balance to throw the opponent.

Tomoe Nage 巴投 (Comma throw)
From the grappling pose called Kumiuchi, you take a step back to unbalance the opponent, you put one foot inside the opponent's legs, then you put the other foot on the base of the thigh and there you drop with the whole body to the ground throwing the opponent over yourself.

Tachi Nagare 立流 (Stand flow)
From the grappling pose called Kumiuchi, throw the opponent literally by throwing yourself under his legs by doing the technique Tachi Nagare from Ukemi Gata.

Yoko Nagare 横流 (Side flow)
From the grappling pose called Kumiuchi, throw the opponent literally throwing yourself to the side of your legs by doing the technique Yoko Nagare from Ukemi Gata.

Temakura 手枕 (Hand cushion)

From the grappling pose called Kumiuchi, you take a back step to extend the opponent's arm and you pass your right arm under the opponent arm with the hand to the back of your head as a cushion putting the forearm edge in order to make a lever to the opponent arm, from this position you drop your weight sweeping the opponent foot so that the opponent can break the shoulder in the fall, once on the ground you can put a lever to control him to the ground.

Kuruma Nage 車投 (Wheel throw)

From the grappling pose called Kumiuchi, you take a step back to unbalance the opponent, you put one foot inside the opponent's legs, then you put the other foot on the base of the thigh and there you drop with the whole body to the ground throwing the opponent over yourself, continuing the movement you do a Koho Kaiten finishing on to the opponent at this point you do a Honjime to control him on the ground.

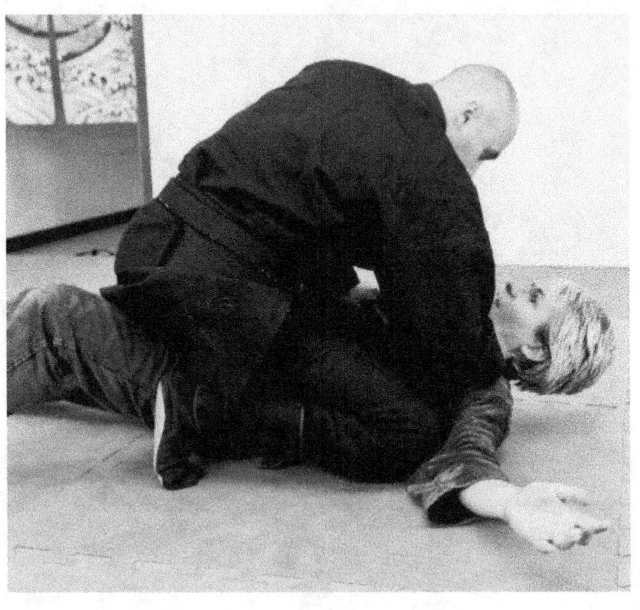

空気投

Kuki Nage

"The quintessence of the throw is Kuki Nage "aerial throw" which is to throw an opponent without touching him. "The clouds are unaware that they are moving and in which direction they are going, but nevertheless it move and can't be grasped."

Soke Masaaki Hatsumi

GYAKU WAZA
(Joint-lock and leverage techniques)

When the opponent grab the left lapel, a person who has studied Kobudo 古武道 (the ancient martial arts) would check the grab with his hand using the metacarp of the little finger, that meaning, use the palm of his hand on the opponent's right hand use the edge of the hand on the beginning of the wrist, to control the grab is very important to prevent attacks from the opponent and to be able to perform a Gyaku with appropriate time.

The Gyaku Waza can be practiced also by taking the sleeve or wrist. When making Gyaku Waza you should practice without using the strength, making sure that the Gyaku might have an impact on the whole body through the spine.

Take Ori 竹折 (Break the Bamboo)
These techniques consist especially in the compression of wrist by bending it, and it can be applied in various ways.

- Omote Take Ori 表竹折 (External break the bamboo)

You grab the back of the opponent's hand and bend the wrist toward the inside of the forearm.

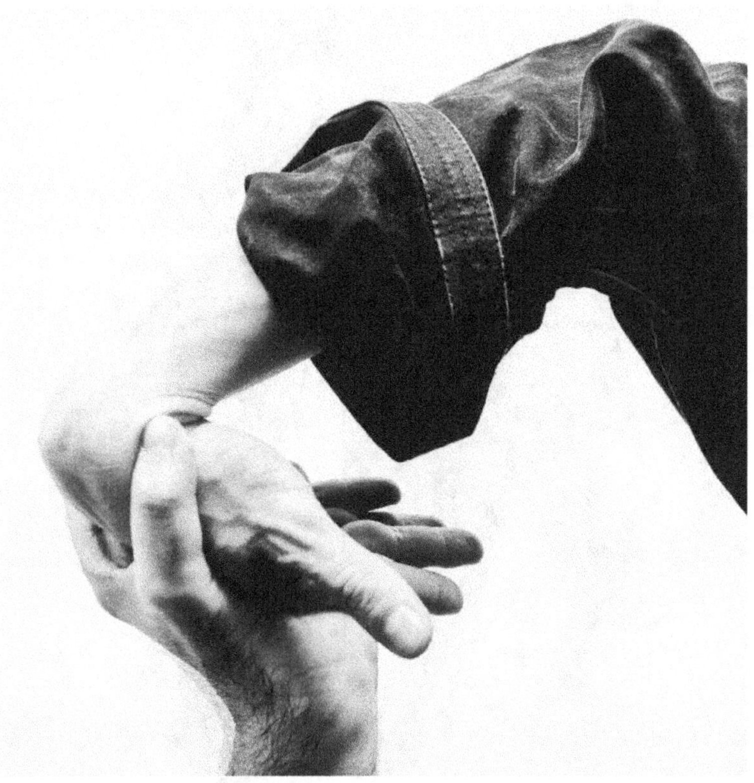

- Ura Take Ori 裏竹折 (Internal break the bamboo)

You grab the opponent's palm and bend the wrist toward the inside of the forearm.

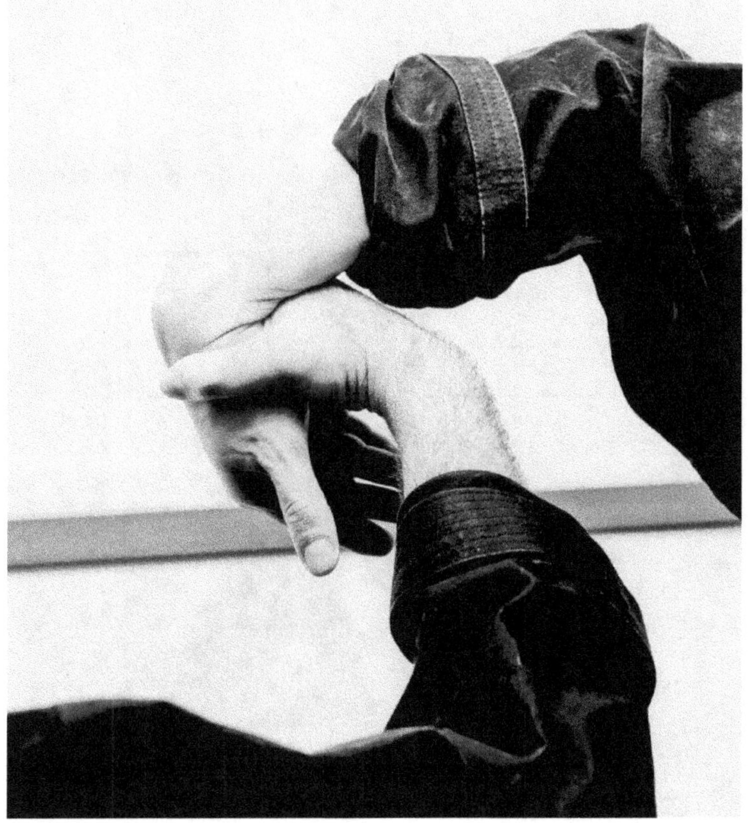

- Omote Gyaku Take Ori 表逆竹折 (Externaljoint-lock break the bamboo)

You grab the back of the opponent's hand and bend the wrist toward the inside twisting it.

- Ura Gyaku Take Ori 裏逆竹折 (Internal joint-lock break the bamboo)

You grab the opponent's palm and bend the wrist toward the inside of the forearm twisting it.

- Omote Take Ori Taidori 表竹折体捕 (Externalbreak the bamboo with the body)

You grab the back of the opponent's hand and bend the wrist toward the inside of the forearm, and place his elbow on your chest.

- Ura Take Ori Taidori 裏竹折体捕 (Internal break the bamboo with the body)

You grab the opponent's palm and bend the wrist toward the inside of the forearm, putting the back of his hand on your chest and with your other hand push on the elbow.

Omote Gyaku Roppo 表逆六法 (Externaljoint-lock six methods)

The opponent grabs the collar with one hand "Katamunedori" 片胸捕, from the natural position you control the opponent's grab, you unbalance him and freeing the collar from his hand, you thrown him to the ground with Omote Gyaku, and performing the following joint-locks: 1) twist his wrist in Omote Gyaku pressing with the tibia on the opponent's arm arching him, 2) put the opponent on his side and insert your right foot edge on the opponent's throat and twists the arm on the right of the tibia, 3) you put the edge of the left foot under the armpit and twist the arm on the left tibia, 4) go down on your knees putting a take Ori while kicking with the foot tip on the opponent's ribs, 5) you put your knee on the biceps of the opponent (Itami Osae 痛み押ちえ "painful pressure control on the ground") while twisting the wrist Omote Gyaku, 6) performing a Zenpo Kaiten over the opponent.

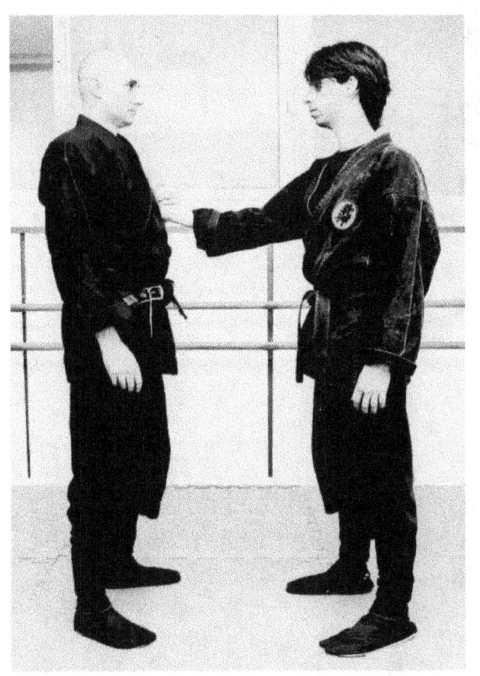

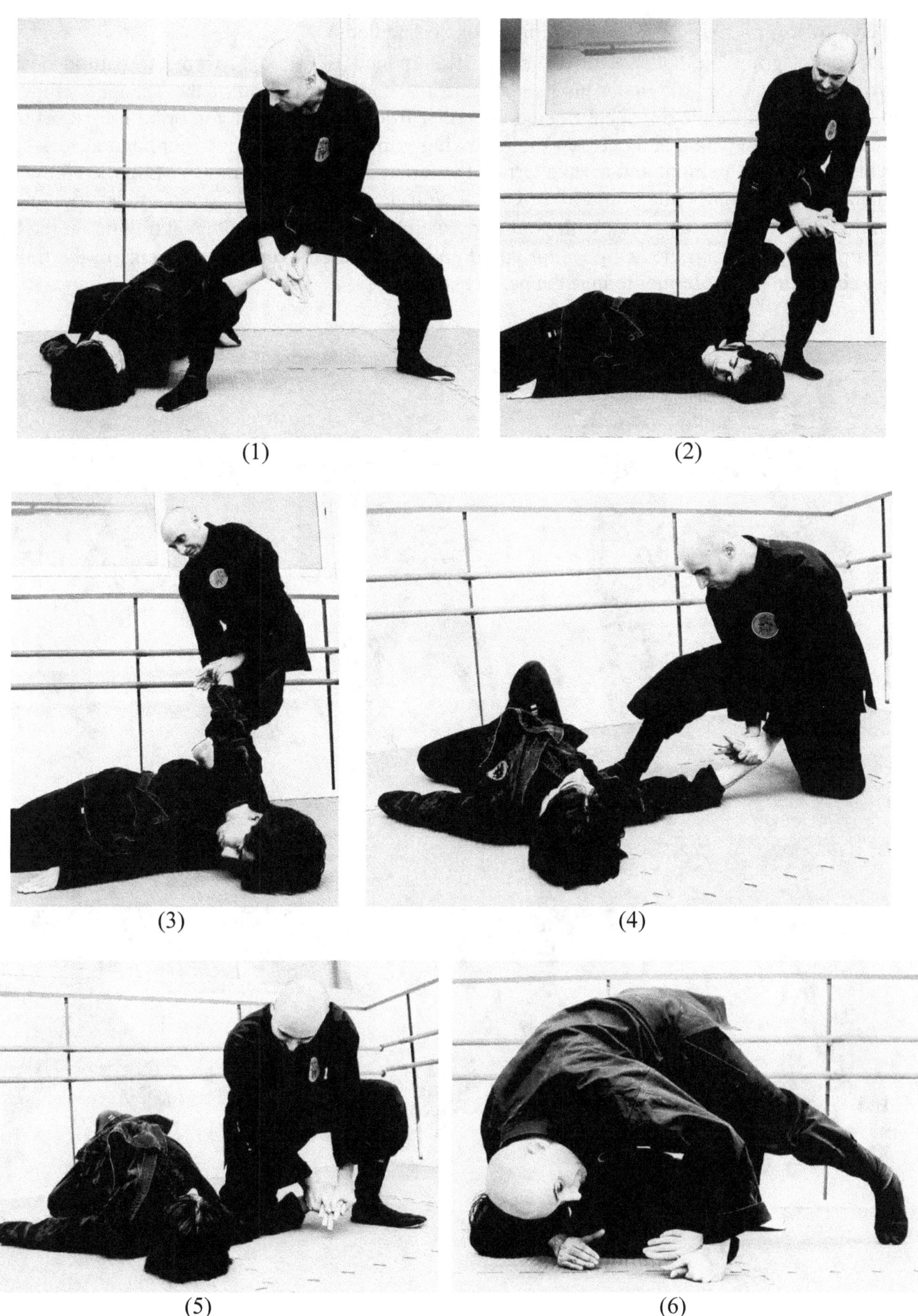

(1)   (2)

(3)   (4)

(5)   (6)

Ura Gyaku Roppo 裏逆六法 (Internal joint-lock six methods)

The opponent grabs the collar with one hand "Katamunedori" 片胸捕, from the natural position control the opponent's grab under his hand like in the tradition fashion of the Takagi Yoshin Ryu school, you unbalance the opponent freeing the collar from his hand, and you bring it forward to the ground with a Ura Gyaku, and perform the following joint-lock: 1) you put your hand in fork shape over his shoulder pressing it and a Take Ori on the wrist, 2) extend the arm twisting the elbow with one hand towards you, while you do Ura Gyaku with the other hand 3) do a shoulder torsion Ude Garami 腕搦み, 4) do a Ohgyaku with your body weight, 5) do a Ryote Ohgyaku lying on the back of the opponent, 6) from the last position you do a Koho Kaiten over the opponent (in the training do not complete it in order not to hurt the partner).

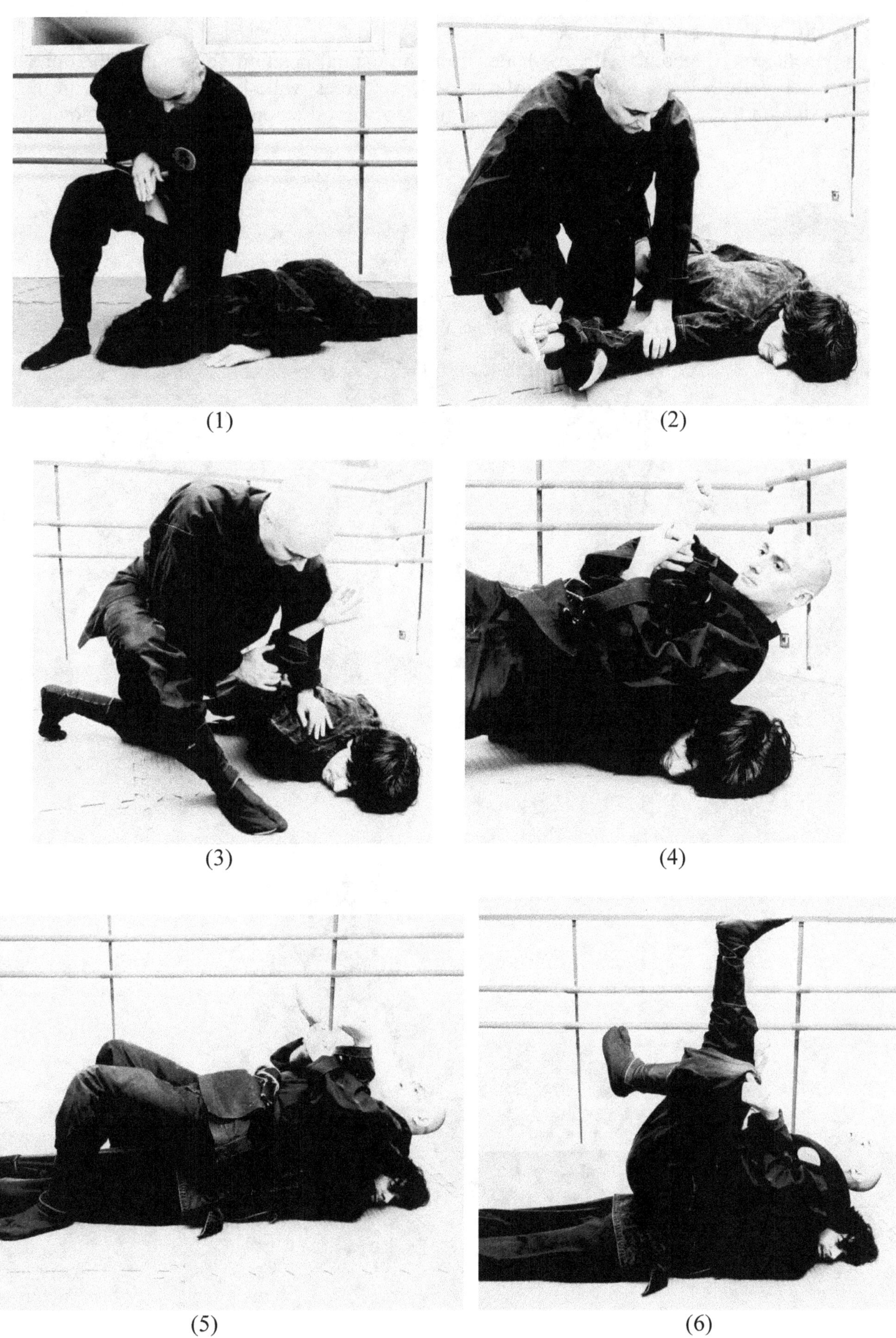

(1) (2) (3) (4) (5) (6)

Hon Gyaku 本逆 (Regular joint-lock)

The opponent grab the collar with one hand, from the natural position you control the opponent's grab and step with the right foot turning the wrist 180 degrees while keeping in line with the arm, you do a step on the same place and bending slightly forward the opponent will kneel down for the pain.

Omote Oni Kudaki 表鬼砕 (External demon smash)

The opponent grab the collar with one hand, from the natural position you control the opponent's grab and unbalance him with a back step, you pass your right arm under and behind your opponent's right triceps and the left arm to the internal trapping the arm as you join your hands, with a rotate step backwards bringing the opponent down to the ground and control him by keeping the join-lock.

Ura Oni Kudaki 裏鬼砕 (Internal demon smash)

The opponent grabs the collar with one hand, from the natural position you check the opponent's grab and unbalance him with a back step, you pass the right arm above the opponent's right bicep and the left arm to the internal trapping the arm as you grab with your hand the left forearm with a rotate step backwards bringing the opponent down to the ground and control him by keeping the join-lock.

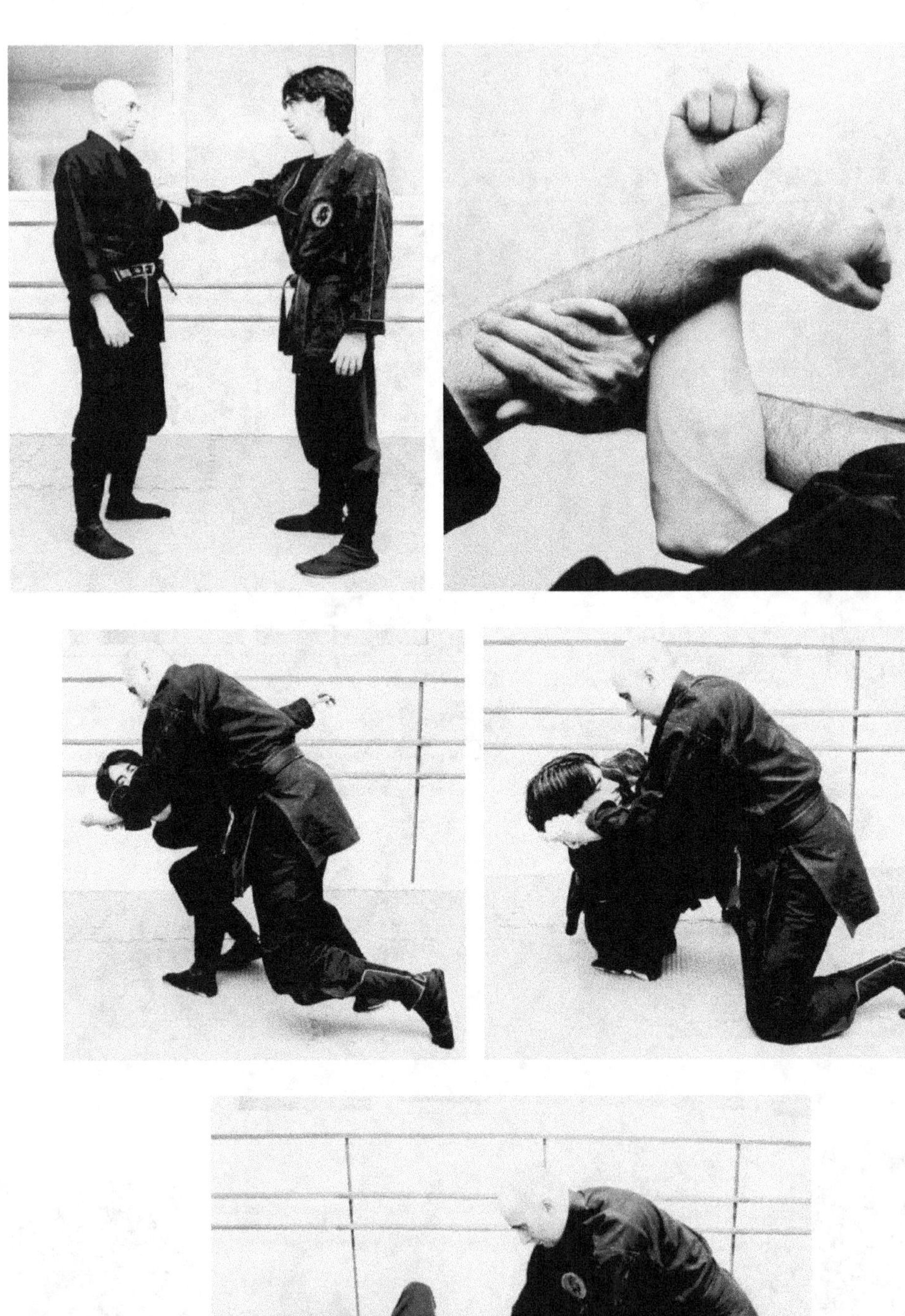

Muso Dori 武双捕 (Capture martial pair)

The opponent grabs the left sleeve with his right hand, from the natural position you unbalance him with a back step, you bring the left hand below the opponent's right elbow, overturn the arm to put it in lever at this point becomes you take a step backward so that the opponent goes down with his face and hits your knee, control him by keeping the lever on the arm.

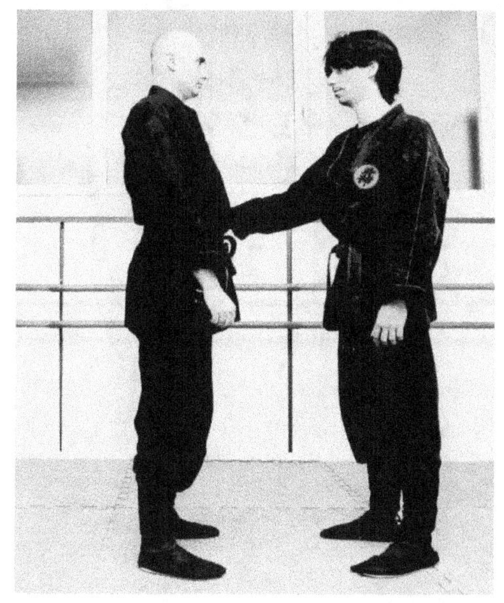

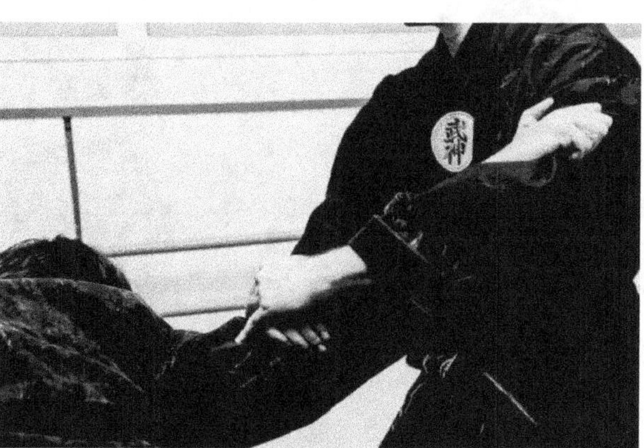

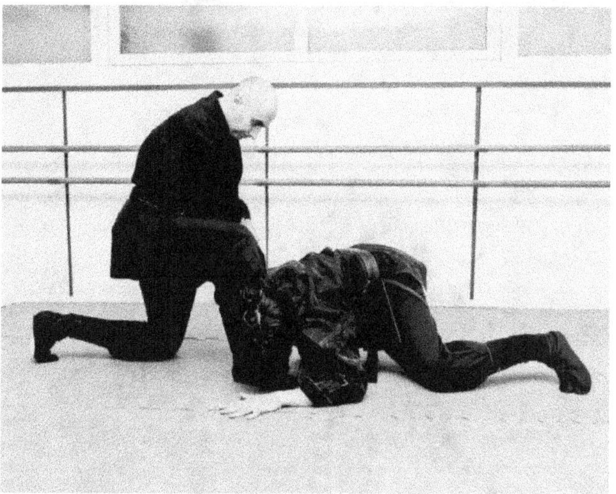

Ohgyaku 大逆 (Big reverse)
The opponent grabs your left wrist with his right hand, from the natural position you unbalance him with a back step, you grab his wrist rotating the arm from the bottom to up and with your right hand grab his right shoulder and pull the opponent down to the ground.

Juji Dori 十字捕 (Cross capture)

The opponent grabs your left sleeve with his right hand, from the natural position you unbalance him with a back step, wrap the opponent's arm from above, the opponent stretch his arm, with your forearm edge push under the elbow and step in with your left leg making a spine rotation to throw the opponent.

SHIME WAZA
(Strangling techniques)

With the strangling techniques, people tend to think about only to squeeze the neck, but there are Shime Wazas for the whole body. For beginners, there is a way to strengthen the neck against the strangulation using the tension of the neck muscles. Traditionally, there was also a training called Kubi Gatame 首固め "fortifying of the neck" using a forked branch, in the training begin allowing a partner to put the branch on your neck and leaving him push, in turn, you push forward with the strength of the neck muscles. However, do not overdo this exercise, there have been cases in which the practitioner broke his neck, you should be very careful in this practice.

The strangling techniques are very dangerous, and you should be very careful in practicing them, you have to start with light pressure and increase it gradually, you must NEVER bring your partner in the unconscious state, you should practice them under the supervision of your teacher that should know the basic techniques of first aid, or the traditional Japanese techniques called Kappo 活法 or Katsu 活 "resuscitation techniques".

Hon Jime 本締み (Regular strangling)
With your left hand you take the opponent's lower left lapel pulling it down, and you put your right hand inside his collar at the top with the thumb outside to grab it, twist your hand choking with the collar and pressing with the forearm edge to strangle the opponent by pressing on the trachea to block his breath.

Gyaku Jime 逆締み (Reverse strangling)
With your left hand you take the opponent's lower left lapel pulling down, and you put your right hand on the outside of the collar at the top with the thumb inside to grab it, twist your hand choking with the collar and pressing with the knuckles on the artery to block the blood flow to the brain.

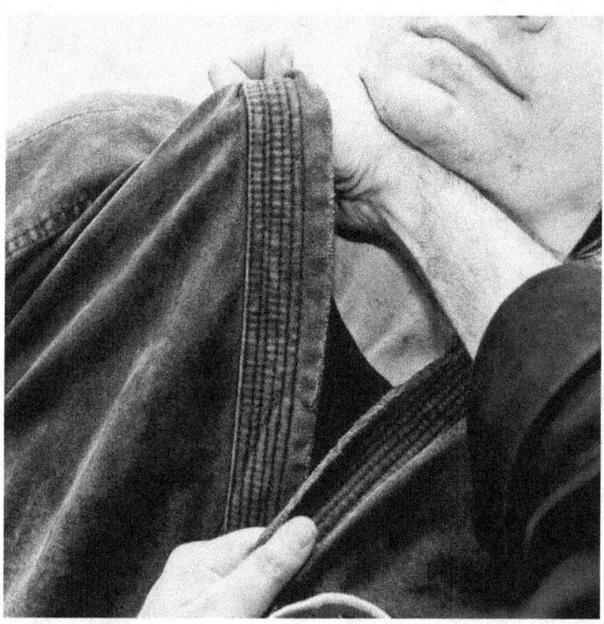

Hon Jime and Gyaku Shime are typical traditional Japanese strangling techniques, because this are performed with the lapels of Keikogi 稽古着 typical Japanese training dress.

Itami Jime 痛締み (Pain strangling)

The strangling technique called Itami Shime or "Pain strangling" consist into strangling using the vital points such as squeezing the trapezius muscles and pressing with your thumbs at points called Ukin and Sakin at lymph glands.

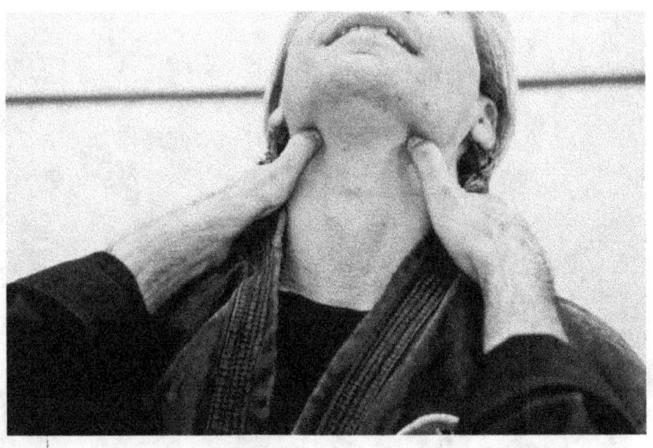

Sankaku Jime 三角締み (Triangle strangling)

Sankaku Jime as the name hints is to form a triangle choke putting your arms in the shape of a triangle, here it is very important the use of forearm edge as you grab your own arms.

Do Jime 胴締み (Trunk strangling)

This technique is to "strangle" or rather squeeze the torso of the opponent with your own legs, to do so you grab the trapezius muscles with both hands and jump on the opponent without falling, performing Ukimi 浮き身 "floating" on him. Traditionally, one could train in this technique even alone using the trunk of a tree.

Henka 変化 (Variation)

人略の巻

Jin Ryaku no Maki
(The scroll of the principle of Man)

意識を伸ばす
Ishiki Wo Nobasu

At the begining, it is natural to focus only on the physical movement, but many people do not go beyond that, and they do not think to train the patience, staying focused only on technique. The longer you wait, the more you let it happen naturally and the easier you will know what will happen next. This is not a conscious observation but being at one with your body and with the universe. In Budo, this is known as "Ishiki wo nobasu" 意識を伸ばす, the expansion or development of awareness, which allows us to perceive what comes next.

SUWARI GATA
(Sitting forms)

Suwari Gata is the generic name for the techniques performed in typical Japanese sitting positions of traditional martial arts, you can train from the positions Fudoza no Kamae, Seiza no Kamae, and from any other position sitting on the ground or even kneel, you should practice by training depending on the circumstances with the three heights as are examples of the three techniques below, according to the three levels Tenchijin 天地人 (Ten 天 heaven rising, Chi 地 earth, lying, Jin 人 man, kneeling).

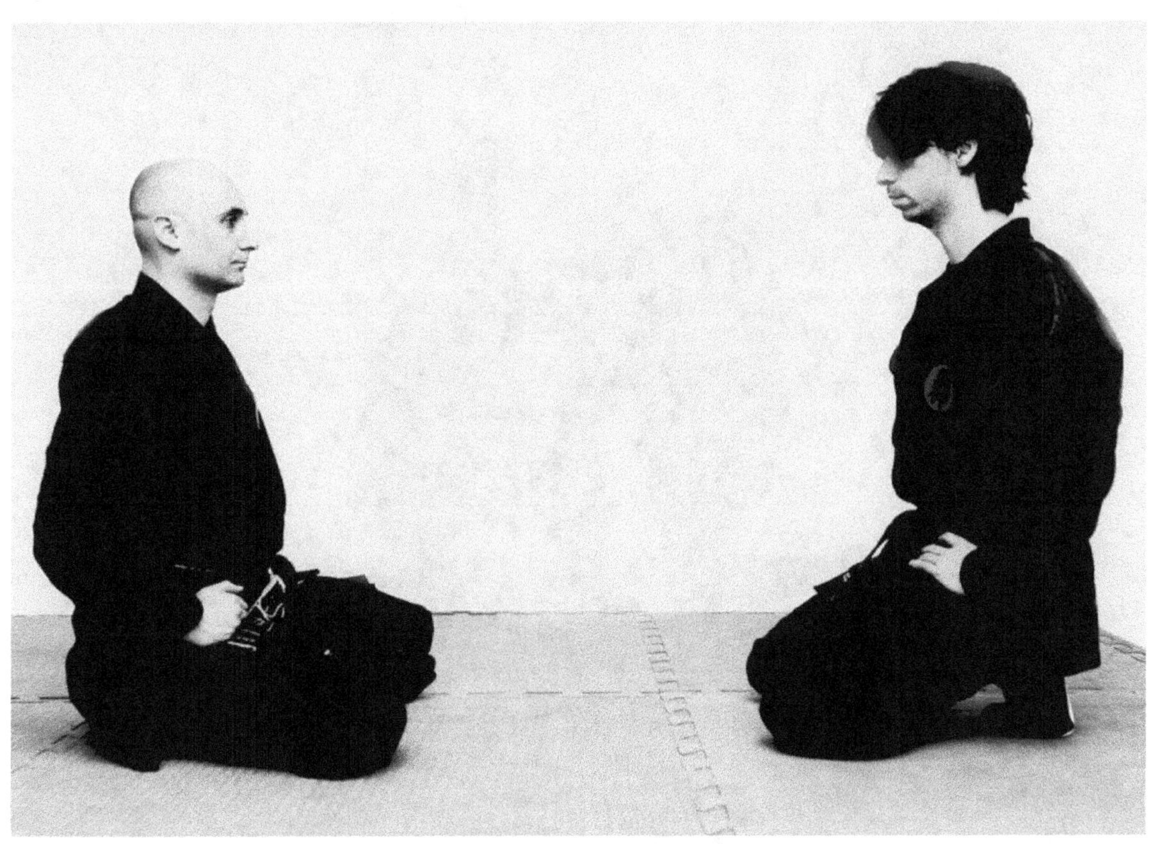

Ichi Geki 一撃 (Blow)

The opponent from Seiza no Kamae gets up on his knees and grabs your collar, from Fudoza no Kamae you control with your left hand, grabbing with the right hand the opponent's right shoulder you hit with Migi Sokugyaku Geri to Suigetsu, you get up backing and hitting with Migi Shuto Ken on the weak point called Nagare to the opponent right arm, "Zanshin".

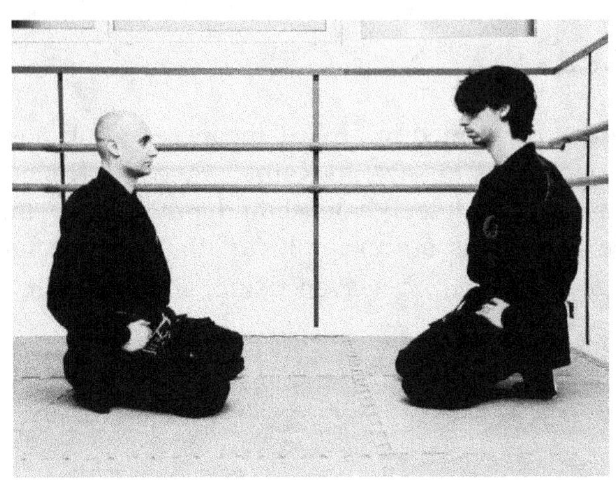
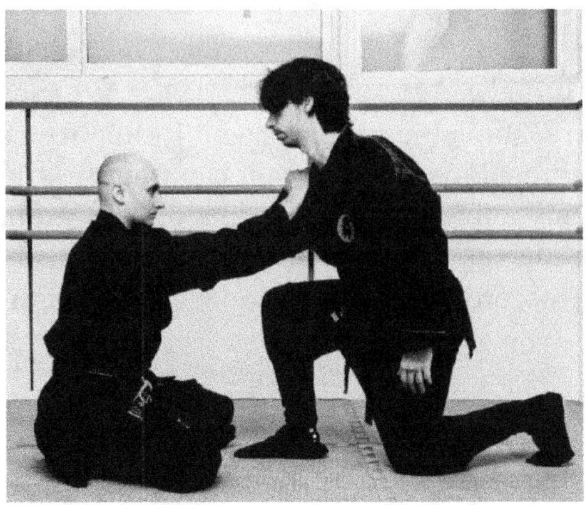

Osae Komi 抑込 (Push in)

The opponent from Seiza no Kamae gets up on his knees and grabs your collar, from Fudoza no Kamae you control with the left hand, you get up with the weight on your left knee to do Hongyaku, and kick with your right foot the opponent left leg to unbalance and bring him to the ground, control with your left knee over his shoulder.

Ude Ori 腕折 (Arm break)

The opponent from Seiza no Kamae gets up on his knees and grabs your collar with his left hand, from Fudoza no Kamae you control with the left hand the grab, by shifting your weight backward and sideways trapping the opponent arm with your legs, put a lever to the arm and a choke with the left leg at the same time.

TSUKI KATA
(Punches form)

Jigoku Otoshi 地獄落 (Fall to hell)

The opponent from Ichimonji no Kamae strikes with Fudo Ken, from Shizen no Kamae you avoid outside and grab the wrist with your right hand and with the other hand on the elbow, turning clockwise lowers the opponent's arm raising the left knee and putting the arm in lever and bringing the opponent to the ground and control him by keeping the knee above the elbow.

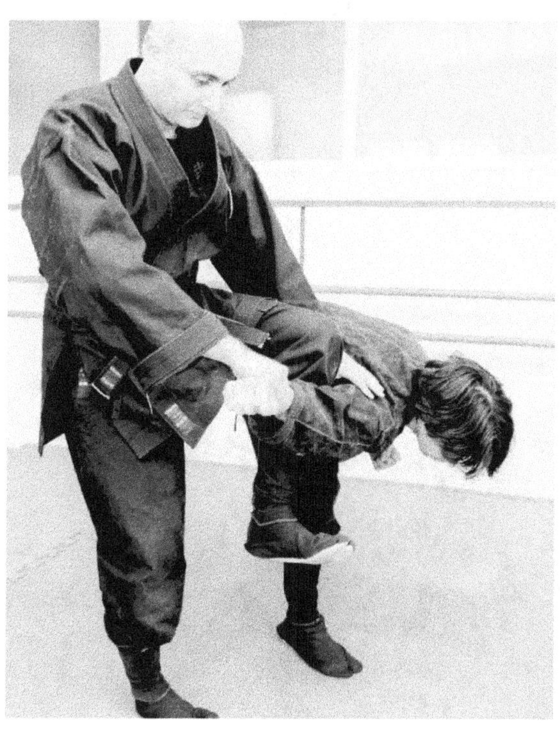
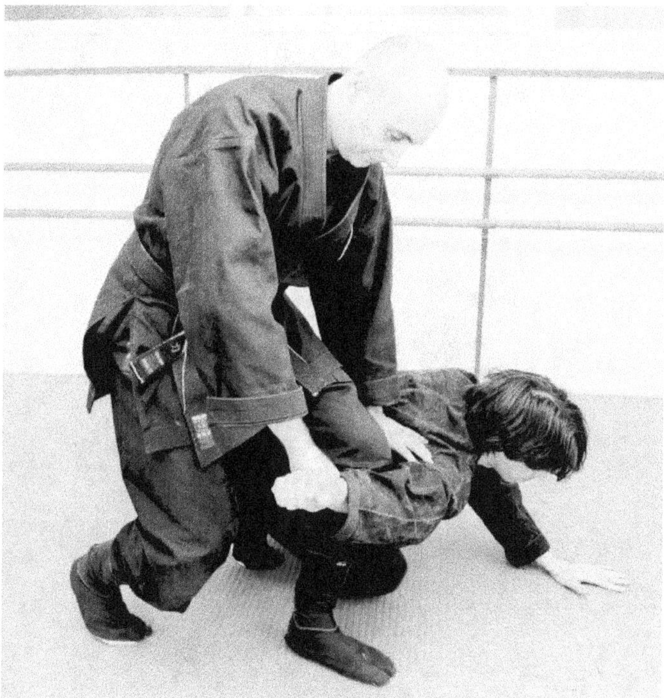

Koyoku 抗抑 (Resist push)

The opponent from Ichimonji no Kamae strikes with Fudo Ken, from Ichimonji no Kamae (by Koto Ryu school) avoid in side doing Nagashi Uke 流し受 ("to receive flowing"), then you hit with the other hand with Fudo Ken to the chin, and throw the opponent with Ganseki Nage.

Hisaku 飛搾 (Jump squeeze)

The opponent from Ichimonji no Kamae strikes with Fudo Ken, from Ichimonji no Kamae (by Koto Ryu school) you do a Jodan Uke and you hit with Boshi Ken in the vital point on the neck called Uko, you grab the trapezius muscles jumping on the opponent performing a Dojime, you slide down and grab the opponent ankles knocking him backward. You control one leg pressing with your forearm on the weak point called "Kobura" and you hit with Kakato Ken 踵拳 (heel kick) to the solar plexus.

Setsu Yaku 雪耀 (Snow twinkle)

The opponent from Ichimonji no Kamae strike with Fudo Ken, from Shizen no Kamae do a Sukui
Uke 掬受 ("to receive spoon shape") with your left hand and twists the wrist, you pass the right arm
under the opponent's arm pressing with the forearm edge doing a lever, when the opponent is up on
his toes with your right hand grab the collar behind the shoulder of the opponent and stepping with
the right foot knock him to the ground.

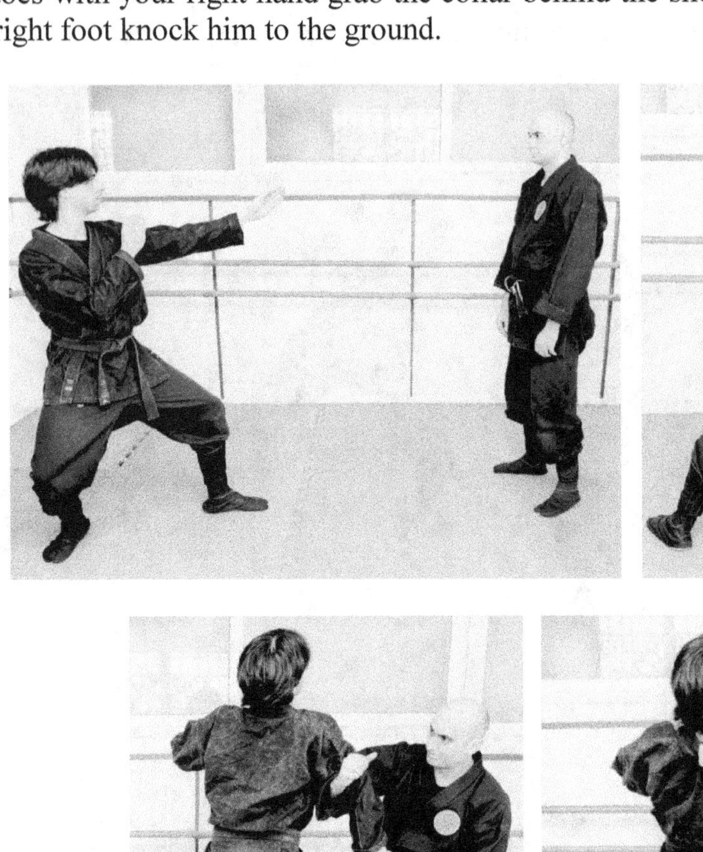

Musan 霧散 (Vanishing)

The opponent from Ichimonji no Kamae strikes with Fudo Ken to the solar plexus "Suigetsu", from Shizen no Kamae grab his wrist with your left hand and hit with Fudo Ken to the face, and then hit with Shuki Ken in "Butsumetsu" pass under the opponent arm putting the arm in lever and strike the arm with Omote Shuto Ken.

Gekkan 月肝 (Moon spirit)

The opponent from Ichimonji no Kamae strikes with Fudo Ken, from Shizen no Kamae do a Sukui Uke with your left hand and take the wrist, with your right hand grab the opponent's right shoulder and kick with the right foot in the Suigetsu while performing Ohgyaku at the same time you kneel on you right leg. You control keeping the lever on the shoulder.

Katamaki 片巻 (One-side wrap)

The opponent from Ichimonji no Kamae strikes with right and then left Fudo Ken. From Ichimonji no Kamae (by Koto Ryu school) you do a Jodan Uke to his right fist, while for the left fist you do a Nagashi Uke with your right hand and wrap his right arm clockwise, you hit with the left Boshi Ken in Butsumetsu, and bring him down.

Unjaku 雲雀 (Skylark) [This ideograms can reads also as Hibari]
The opponent from Ichimonji no Kamae strikes with Fudo Ken, from Shizen no Kamae go down on your knee with both hands touching the ground in front of the opponent. Suddenly, with the right hand strike with Fudo Ken in "Asagasumi" and taking advantage of the opening created you do a Ganseki Otoshi.

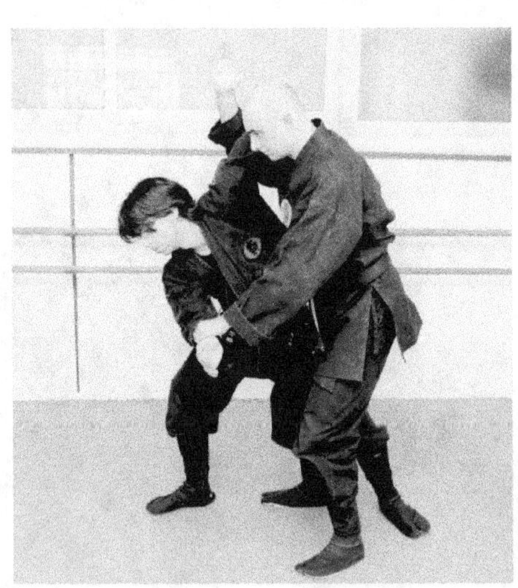

Shiho Dori 四方捕 (Four direction capture)

The opponent from Ichimonji no Kamae strikes with right Fudo Ken. You from Shizen no Kamae do a Jodan Uke with your left hand. The opponent strikes again with left Fudo Ken. You do a Jodan Uke with your right hand, the opponent strike you again with right Fudo Ken.You do a Nagashi Uke with your left hand and do the technique Ura Onikudaki. The opponent stretch his arm out to use it as a counter-technique, using his reaction strike with Migi Ura Shuto Ken in Uko and grab his right shoulder and kick to Suigetsu and take him to the ground and then control him.

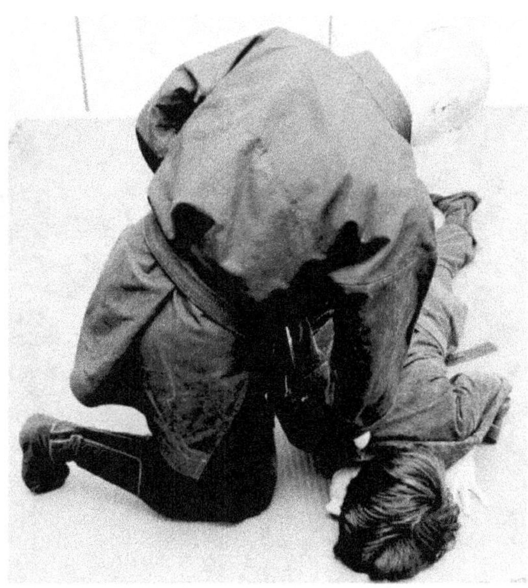

Moguri Dori 潜捕 (Submerge capture)

The opponent from Ichimonji no Kamae strikes with right Fudo Ken. From Shizen no Kamae you do a Jodan Uke with your left hand. The opponent attacks again with left Fudo Ken. You do a Jodan Uke with your right hand, the opponent attacks again with right Fudo Ken. You do a Jodan Uke with your left hand and hit him with Fudo Ken to the arm's weak point called Jakkotsu, and passing under the arm, you throw the opponent to the floor with Ganseki Otoshi.

Ken Nagare 拳流 (Punch flow) [Also known as Ken Nagashi]
The opponent from Ichimonji no Kamae strikes with a very strong right Fudo Ken, from Shizen no Kamae avoid it externally absorbing "Aigamae" 和構 (absorbing posture), grab the wrist of the opponent's punch with your right hand throwing the opponent, he will throw himself for the excessive strength in his punch.

Jumonji 十文字 (Cross shape)

The opponent from Ichimonji no Kamae strikes with right Fudo Ken, from Shizen no Kamae you do a Jodan Uke followed immediately by a Migi Fudo Ken to the opponent right biceps, and then hit with a left Boshi Ken in opponent's Butsumetsu.

Kappi 括飛 (To bind and jump)
You approach to the opponent and at the right time you strike with right Ura Shuto Ken to opponent's right Uko, after you strike again with left Ura Shuto Ken hitting the left Uko then suddenly jump back and then Zanshin.

151

Konpi 梱飛 (To tie up and jump)

You approach to the opponent and at the right time you strike with left Ura Shuto Ken to opponent's right Uko, then suddenly you jump to the right side and then Zanshin.

間合

Maai

"You've got to learn to utilize the space between you and your opponent. Distancing, angling and timing are very important."

Soke Masaaki Hatsumi

KERI GAESHI GATA
(Counter-kicks form)

Huko 夫虚 (Man false)
The opponent strikes with Migi Zempo Geri, from Shizen no Kamae avoid it and hit with Fudo Ken to the thigh and knock down the opponent hitting with Suihei Geri to the other leg.

Ketaoshi 桁落 (Kick and knock down)

The opponent strikes with Migi Zempo Geri, you from Shizen no Kamae avoid inside and kick with Sokugyaku Geri to the groin, kneeling hit with Shuki Ken in the opponent knee joint, and by grabbing with double Shako Ken to fluctuating ribs throw the opponent with Yoko Nagare.

Ashi Dome 足止 (Stop the foot)

The opponent strikes with Migi Zempo Geri, from Shizen no Kamae avoid the outside and passing under the leg lock the supporting leg with the left foot with "Ashirau" and knock down the opponent.

Geri Sukui 蹴掬 (Spoon kick)

The opponent strikes with Migi Jodan Mawashi Sokko Geri, from Shizen no Kamae avoid by lowering and sweep the support leg with a counterclockwise rotation kick knock down the opponent.

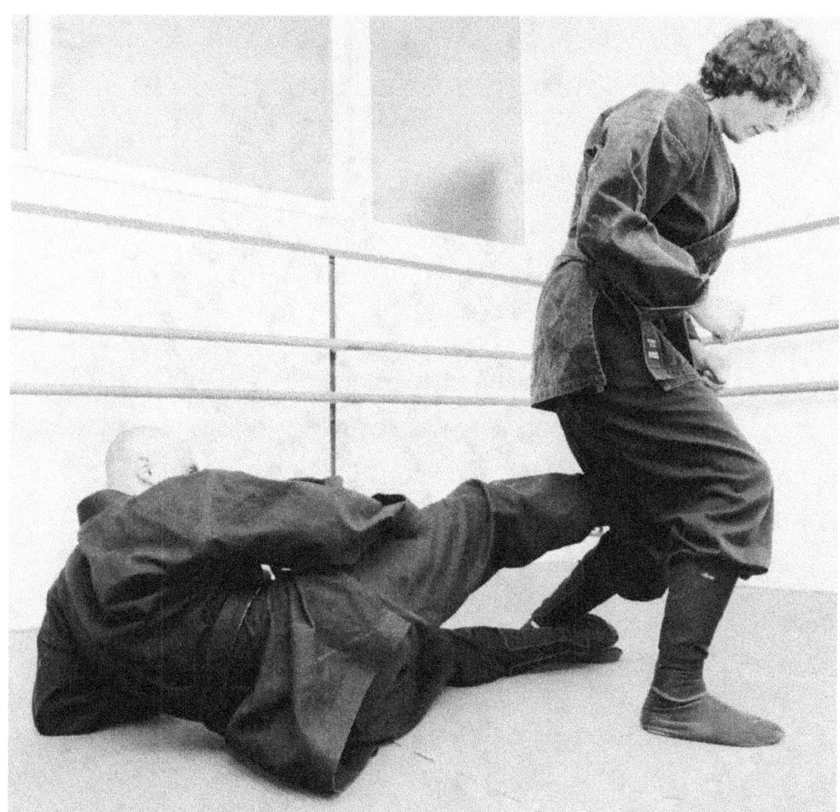

(You can also perform a scissor movement at the support leg)

Jigoku Otoshi 地極落 (Fall to hell)

The opponent strikes with Migi Zempo Geri, from Shizen no Kamae avoid outside and grab the ankle with your right hand and the thigh with your left hand, performing a lever on the knee with your left knee, bringing the opponent to the ground.

Kyoto 虚倒 (False fall)

The opponent strikes with Migi Zempo Geri, from Shizen no Kamae avoid and blocking from the outside with Gedan Jumonji Uke 下段十文字受, turning the leg clockwise and pulling it back to you, bring your opponent to the ground and hit with Omote Shuto Ken to the Kobura.

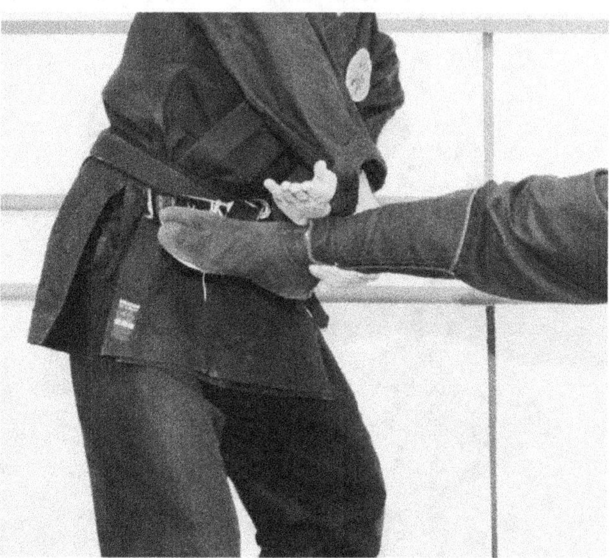

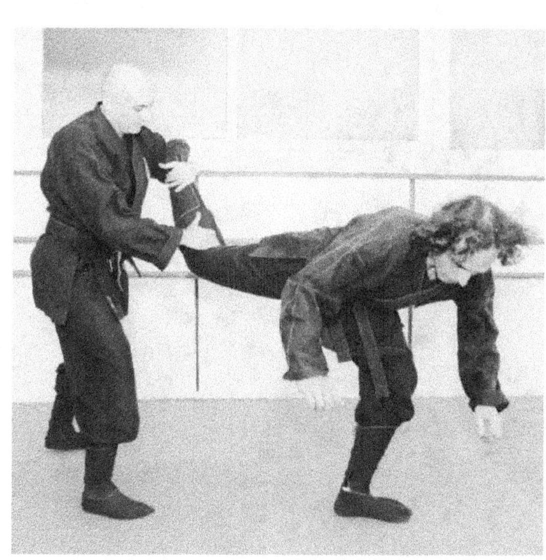

Keto 闕倒 (Imperial palace fall)
The opponent strikes with Migi Zempo Geri, from Shizen no Kamae avoid inside to kick with your right leg under the opponent's leg, the opponent avoids your kick and strikes with right Fudo Ken. Do a Jodan Uke with your left arm and immediately hit the opponent's face with Shako Ken while at the same time you kick with the right leg knocking him down, Zanshin.

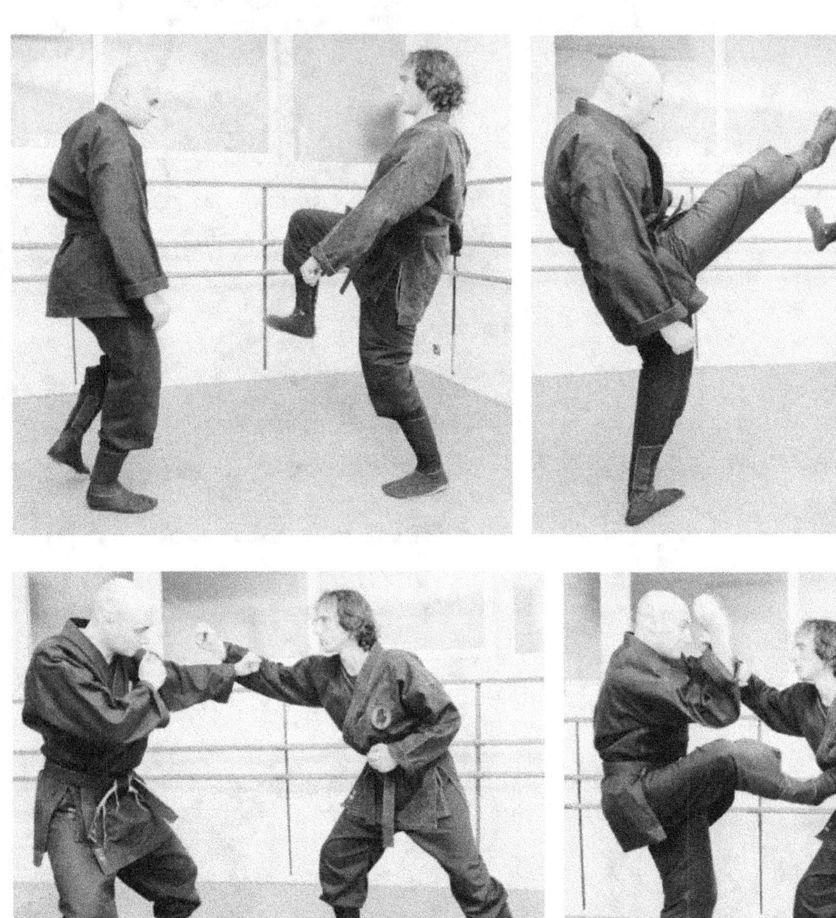

片手捕型

KATATE DORI GATA
(One hand grab form)

Ate Nage 當投 (Bear throw)
The opponent grabs your collar with his left hand, from Shizen no Kamae control the grab and doing a step you hit with Hidari Fudo Ken to the Suigetsu with your right hand while you do Omote Take Ori, pass under the opponent's arm and grab with the other hand above his elbow joint and putting it in lever, with the foot sweep the opponent's left foot to knock him down.

Setto 折倒 (Break and overthrow)
The opponent grabs your collar with his right hand, from Shizen no Kamae control the grab and hit with Migi Fudo Ken to Jakkotsu to break free from the grab and then hit with Hidari Boshi Ken into Butsumetsu.

Hiki Otoshi 引落 (Pull and come down)
The opponent grabs your sleeve over your left shoulder with his right hand, from Shizen no Kamae pull with the forearm edge on opponent's left forearm near the wrist, and pull back kneeling on the right leg and turning to bring the opponent to the ground.

Hito 飛倒 (Jump and overthrow)
The opponent is walking in front of you, you stop him touching his shoulder and when he turns you strike with right Sanshitan Ken in left Ura Kimon, using his reaction you hit again the opponent with Ryoashi Tobi Geri and land on Tatami performing Koho Kaiten, and Zanshin.

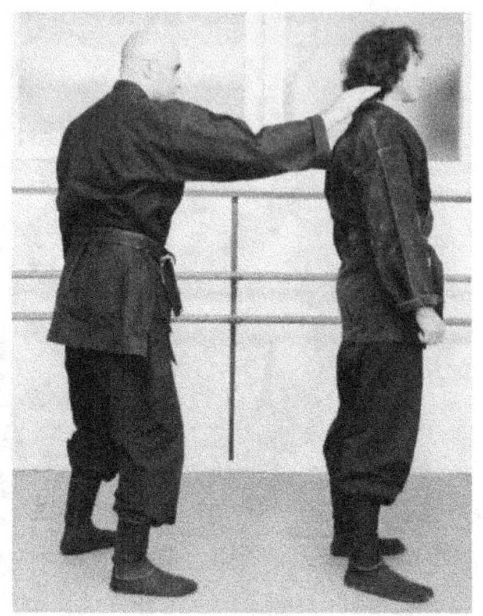

Hoteki 放擲 (Giving up)

The opponent grabs your collar with his left hand, from Shizen no Kamae control his grab, the opponent strikes with right Fudo Ken. You avoid and hit with Hidari Shuto Ken to the point of the arm called "Ura Hoshi". Changing the grab with your right thumb push in "Omote Hoshi" on the opponent's left arm with the other hand twist the wrist and throw with Katate Gyaku Nage (this kind of throw is also called Hane Age 羽上 "raise the wing").

Fudo 不動 (Imperturbable)

The opponent grabs your collar with his left hand, from Shizen no Kamae control his grip with your right hand. The opponent strike with a right Fudo Ken, you do Nagashi Uke with your left hand do a Omote Takeori to his right hand, pass under the opponent's arm with your left hand grab his left shoulder, step back kneeling, knocking the opponent back on his coccyx.

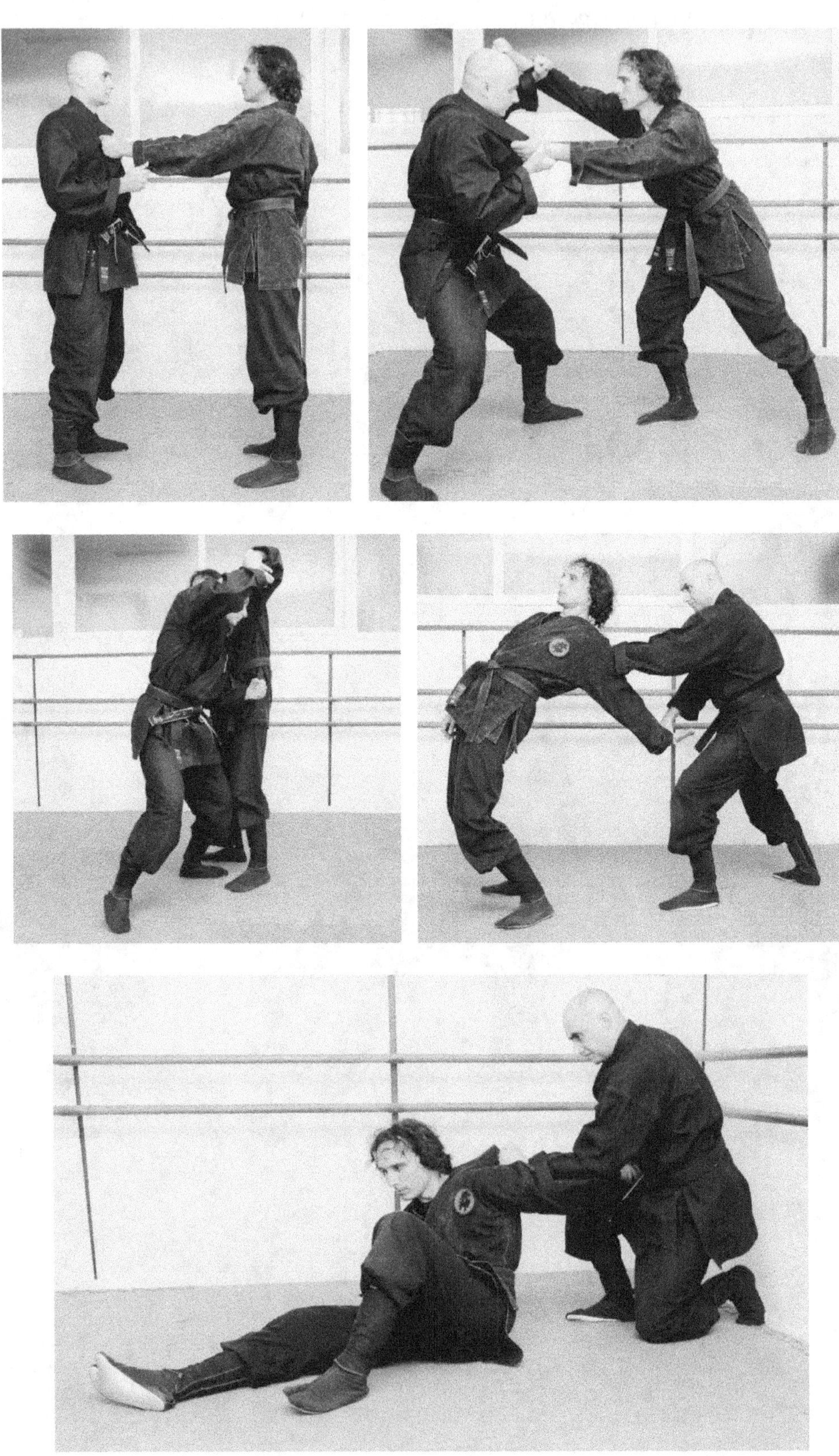

166

Kote Gaeshi 小手返 (Twisting the wrist)
The opponent grabs your left wrist, from Shizen no Kamae grab the opponent's hand and by turning the arm do Ura Gyaku, turning your body bring the opponent to the gound.

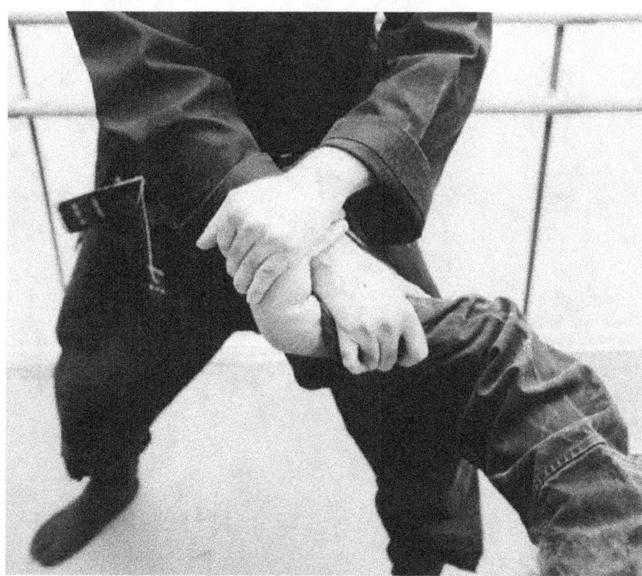

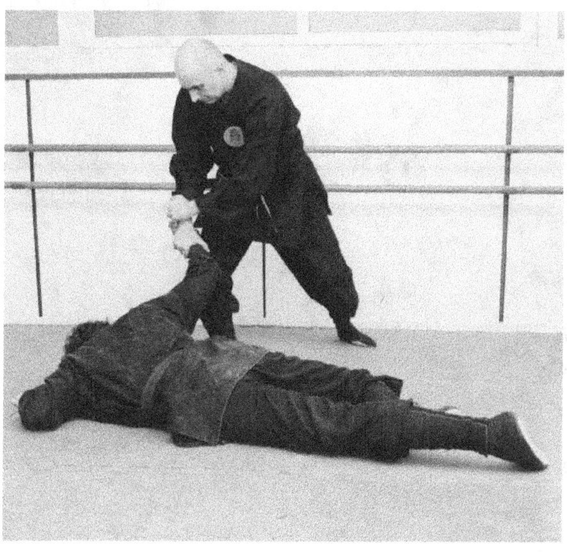

背部寄居型

HAIBU YORI GATA
(Grabs from behind form)

Shisai 指最 (Extremities of the fingers)
The opponent grabs you from behind with his right hand at the collar behind the neck, you from Shizen no Kamae check his grab with your right hand, turn to face the opponent and hit him on the chest with Seiken in Omote Kimon, and do Ura Gyaku to the hand that was grabbing the collar with your left hand on the opponent's elbow, kick with Migi Sokugyaku Geri to Suigetsu and bring the opponent to the ground by kneeling.

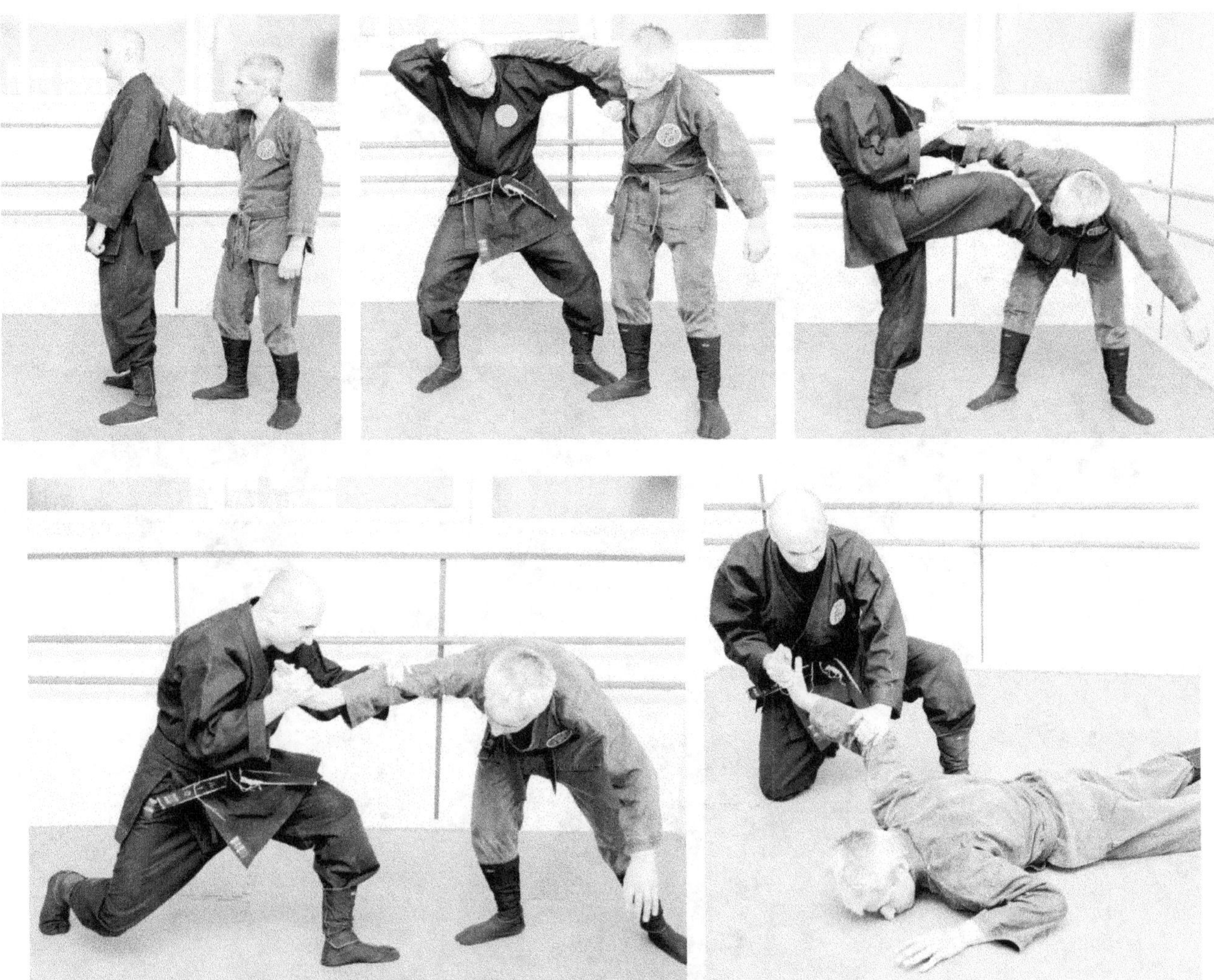

Sakketsu 跳枇 (Leap spoon)

The opponent grabs you from behind squeezing your arms and torso, you from Shizen no Kamae lower your hips and opening his arms hit by pulling back the head, with the right hand grab his right arm and hit with Hidari Seiken to Asagasumi and do Ganseki Nage.

Teiken 蹄拳 (Hoof fist)

The opponent grabs you from behind and under your arms blocking them, you from Shizen no Kamae open the opponent hands by pressing with both Boshiken in the points of the hands called Gokoku, and shifting your weight on the right leg cross the opponent's arms and throw him.

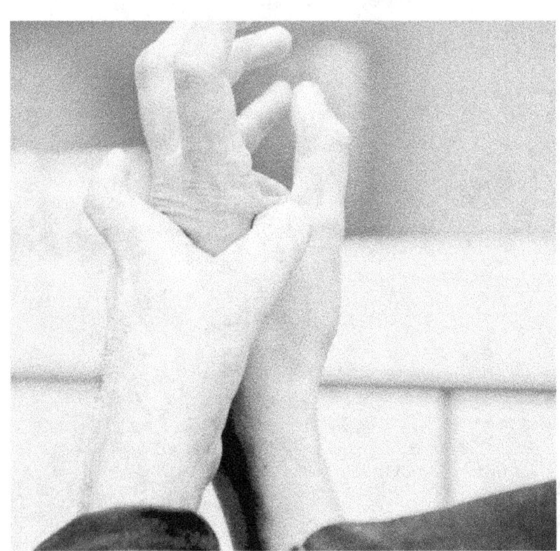

Kinkudaki 睾砕 (Testicles smash)

The opponent grabs you from behind squeezing your arms and torso, you from Shizen no Kamae lower your hips opening his arms and pull the head back and hit with Osae Geri at the point of the foot called Toki, then you hit with Shako Ken in the genitals, once free you throw the opponent with Itami Nage.

Ketsumyaku 締脈 (Vein choke)

The opponent does a Sankaku Jime, you from Shizen no Kamae to prevent strangulation do Kubigatame, then do a pressure on the nerve points with Boshiken in the opponent's elbow, after opening the arm throw the opponent with Katate Gyaku Seoinage.

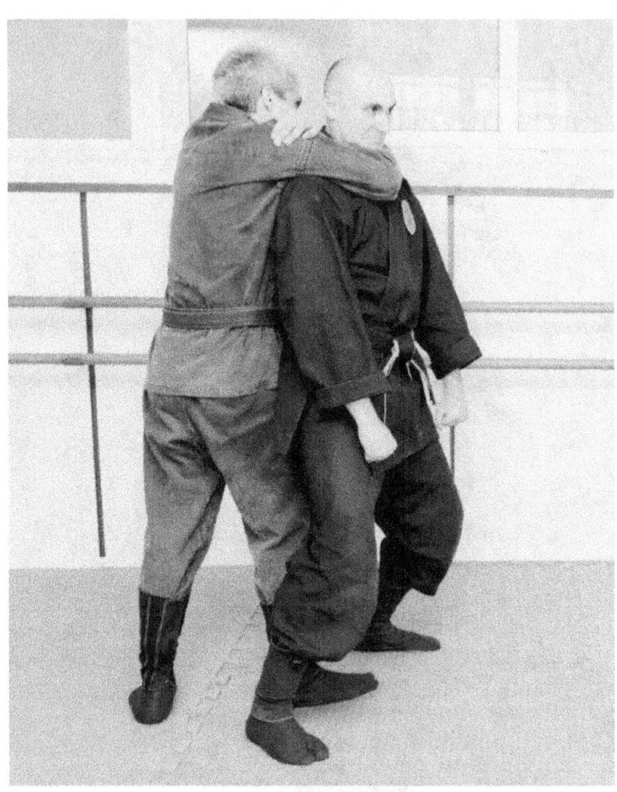

Hanebi 跳火 (Leap up fire)

The opponent grabs you from behind with his right hand at the collar behind the neck, from Shizen no Kamae control the opponent's grab with the right hand, you turn to face the opponent, who strikes in the abdomen with the right kick, you do a Hidari Gedan Uke and then an Ura Gyaku at the hand that grab your collar, then change it in Omote Gyaku and kick while you bring the opponent to the floor with the joint-lock.

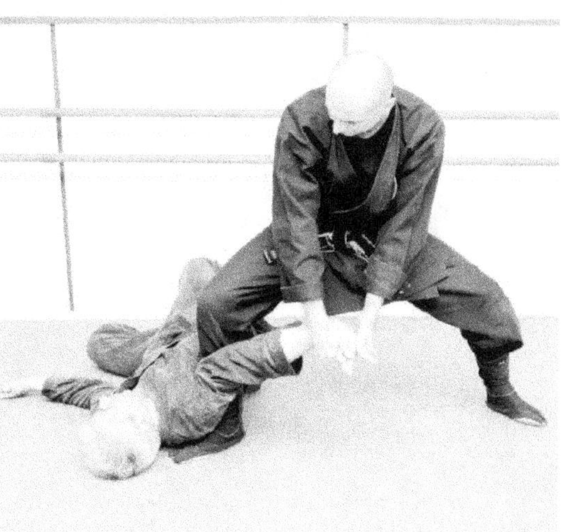

万変変化

Banpen Henka

"For each technique that you learn, you need to understand that it is possible to make 10,000 (endless) changes 'Banpen Henka' 万変変化."

Soke Masaaki Hatsumi

鼠逃遁甲の型

(Evasion protection of the rat escape form)

The ideogram San 鼠 "rat" sounds like the ideogram San 戦 "fight", Tou 逃 escape sounds like "Tou" 跳 run and jump. These Kata are a set of techniques of Ninpo Taijutsu 忍法体術 (Ninja fight techniques) and Tongyo 遁形 (evasion techniques), they are created by Takamatsu Toshitsugu to train beginners in Ninpo. When practicing this form you should always have with you the Shuriken 手裏剣 and metsubushi 目潰し inside Shinobi Shozoku 忍び装束 (Ninja outfit).

銛盤手裏剣

Senban Shuriken

The Togakure Ryu Ninja used various kinds of Shuriken 手裏剣 (throwing blades of various types). The mainly used within this Ryuha were Senban Shuriken developed from Teppan 鉄板 "steel plate", is a four-pointed star, usually with a square hole in the center, the Ninja usually carried with him nine Shurikens.

目潰し

Metsubushi

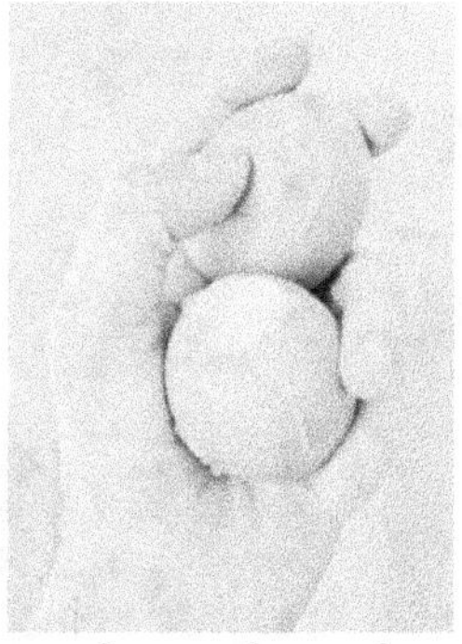

The Metsubushi or "blinding powder" consist to launch a number of substances at the opponent, especially to the face or eyes. This, provides a moment of hesitation, a more than sufficient time for the Ninja to strike, or to escape. The latter action has given rise to legends that the Ninja could disappear "in a cloud of smoke." The Metsubushi to be transported could be made of eggshells or nuts.

Migi Kata Ude Tonso Gata 右片腕遁走型
(Evasion of only right arm form)
You and the opponent are in Hachimonji no Kamae 八文字の構, the opponent grabs your right hand with his right hand, and takes three steps in Yoko Aruki pulling you back to him. Let yourself be pulled doing Yoko Aruki and at the third step you take the wrist in Ura Take Ori raising his arm and kick in the groin with your right leg. Than pass under the opponent's arm and throw with Katate Nage, once the opponent is on the ground you throw a Metsubushi and escape with Mokutonjutsu 木遁術 (evasion by using the wood element).

Sayu Tonso Gata 左右遁走型
(Evasion of right-left form)
You and the opponent are in Hachimonji no Kamae, the opponent grabs your left hand with his right hand, and takes three steps in Yoko Aruki pulling back to him. Let yourself be pulled doing Yoko Aruki and at the third step you take the wrist, raising his arm, and kick in the groin with the right leg, you do a Ohgyaku and step back kneeling bring the opponent to the ground, launch Metsubushi and escape with Mokutonjutsu.

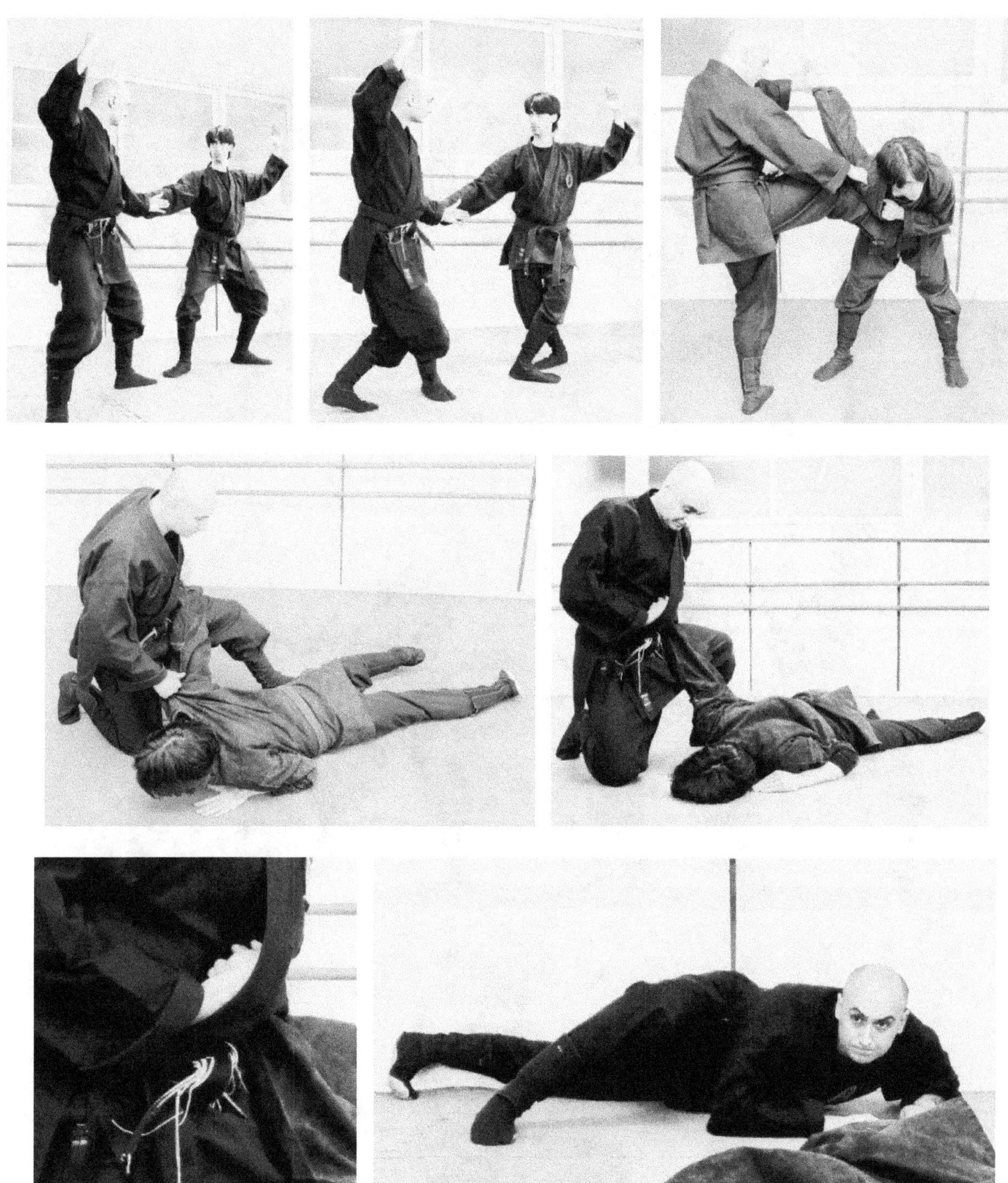

Migi Tekubisuji Tonso no Kata 右手首筋遁走
(Evasion of right wrist form)
The opponent grabs you from behind with his right hand to the collar behind the neck and pulls you to him doing three steps, from Shizen no Kamae let him pull at the third step strike the opponent's foot and control the grab with your right hand, then you turn to face the opponent hitting him with Shukiken at the ribs, and do Ura Gyaku to the hand that was grabbing the collar, grab his left hand on the elbow and throw the opponent with Katate Nage, throw a Metsubushi and escape with Mokutonjutsu.

Ate Komi Tonso Gata 当込遁走型

(Evasion by hitting inside form)

The opponent is armed with a Katana in Daijodan no Kamae, and cuts with Shomen Giri. From Hachimonji no Kamae, shout a Kiai and jumping in front of him hit with right Boshiken in Suigetsu, after you do a Koho Tobi and escape with Mokutonjutsu.

Kote Uchi Tonso no Kata 小手打遁走型

(Evasion by hitting the forearm form)

The opponent is armed with a Katana in Daijodan no Kamae, and cuts with Shomen Giri. From Hachimonji no Kamae, avoid to left and strike at the forearm with right Omote Shuto Ken. The opponent will lower the sword at the same time you hit with left Boshiken in opponent's right Butsumetsu, then you do a Hidari Yoko Tobi and escape with Mokutonjutsu.

Migi Uchi Tonso no Kata 右打遁走型

(Evasion right hit form)

The opponent is armed with a Katana in Seigan no Kamae, and thrusts with Tsuki. From Happo no Kamae 八法の構, turn the body slightly to the right, and hit at the left forearm with Migi Omote Shuto, and take the end of the Tsuka with your left hand disarming the opponent, you do Yoko Tobi and escape with Mokutonjutsu.

Sayu Kumogakure Gata 左右雲隠型
(To hide behind a cloud right-left form)
Two opponents are approaching from the front one on the right and one to the left with the Katana
in Daijodan no Kamae, about 3.5 m, they advance and cut with Shomen Giri, you form the posture
Happogakure no Kamae 八法隠の構 take two or three steps back, keeping the distance until you
are "cornered", at the appropriate time you throw two Metsubushis and immediately jump in, and
strike the opponents with both Boshiken at their vital point Suigetsu, then do a Zenpo Kaiten twice
forward and escape with Mokutonjutsu.

Kosei Kirigakure Gata 攻勢霧隠型
(Offensive hiding in the fog form)
Three or four opponents are armed with the Katana sword to attack from the front, from about 4.5 m, they approach in Seigan or Jodan. From Tonso no Kamae 遁走の構, while they approach to cut, you throw Teppan, when enemies are retreating throw the Metsubushi, and then Zenpo Kaiten between enemies and escape with Mokutonjutsu.

Happo Kirigakure Gata 八方霧隠れ型
(Eight directions hiding in the fog form)
When surrounded by opponents, you throw the Teppan in front of you and disperses Metsubushi behind. Hidden in the cloud created, you kneel and throw the Teppan in all directions hitting opponents that surround you, and escape with Mokutonjutsu.

忍法体術

Ninpo Taijutsu

The essence of martial arts is self defense Goshinjutsu 護身術. The essence of self protection also appears in Ninpo Taijutsu (better known as Ninjutsu 忍術) that also protects our spirit. Without the proper spirit in the martial arts "Budo" 武道 training it could become a disaster.

武道
Budo

"The Budo is a living thing, it is always evolving. People who do not understand this are just collectors of techniques".

Soke Masaaki Hatsumi

五段　審査

Godan Shinsa
(5th Dan test)

The Godan Shinsha (5th Dan test) which is also known as Sakki Test, "Sakki" 殺気 which means "intention to kill", that is the exam to feel the murderous intent of the opponent.

The test is carried out as follows , in Japan it normally takes place after the training and all those who participated may watch the Sakki Test. The practitioner is sitting on the Tatami with his eyes closed, the Soke or one of Shihan Jugodan (15th Dan) stand behind him with a Fukuro Shinai 袋竹刀 (padded sword), which after due concentration issue murderous intent when striking with the Fukuro Shinai. The candidate to pass the examination must "feel" and roll at a suitable distance to avoid the Fukuro Shinai. The candidate has two attempts, if he starts early for the agitation does not count, and has a chance to try again. The most important thing when doing this test is "not thinking" and "relax". The Sakki Test, is an initiation ceremony through the sixth sense. Traditionally, the test of Sakki was performed with the real sword, and if the student failed, he would die. There is something quite like when the ceramics maker, upon opening the kiln, destroys the pieces of work he dislikes. Soke Masaaki Hatsumi told his Sakki Test as follows:

"I too one day some time ago was sitting in my teacher's room, when he said "Please close your eyes and wait, and whatever happens, make sure not to open them!" Then perceiving that my teacher went down the stairs, I let my guard down a little to the sign that he had disappeared. After several hours, some sort of heavy, pressing strength approached diagonally from behind, and seeing an image of a body split in two, I went into sideways-rolling body movement. Then I had a feeling right from the side, of the head flying, and executed a forward breakfall. As I slowly sat down into a natural Fudoza posture, I heard my teachers voice, saying "Well done, you made it, you may open your eyes now", and when I opened my eyes, there stood Sensei, lowering an unsheathed sword in his right hand. I thought it was strange and I asked explanation of what had happened before, he told me that was Kijutsu 気術 (energy techniques) through the sixth sense, or one may say Shinden no Jutsu 神伝の術; such is the Gokui 極意: "If you think there is something there is nothing, If you think there is nothing there is something"; for the first time the profound words of this teaching sank into my body will all their weight; I was deeply impressed by the nature of the words'spirit. Together with the joy of my eyes opening, I received from my teacher that sword. I was latter told by my teacher that this was a Jujikiri Mumyo no Itto 十字切り 無閠の一刀, and that no-one had gone this far; those words joyfully spoken I remember as if they were said yesterday.

Usually the teacher or the Soke himself propose the student for the Sakki Test, when the student is "ready" , this is a very important thing, this is not an exam to be carried out with the attitude of "try", but must only be done when the student is ready, so it is very important that up to that point the student will be trained in their Dojo along with his teacher Shidoshi or Shihan (so that, in turn, has already been "initiated"), with the feeling of Jissen Gata 実戦型 (form of actual combat). It is very important to train this feeling the most possible, once you have mastered the basics, you should always take care to put it in each Kata (forms), Waza (techniques), Henka (variants) or Oyou (applications). Soke often advises us to practice this feeling during training at the Hombu Dojo, for the student that arrived on the 4th Dan there is a preparation that is made together with his teacher Shidoshi or Shihan.

It is important that when you sit in Seiza and close your eyes, that you relax, even if after all a bit of stirring emotion is understandable, knowing that you should learn to control your agitation and emotion, understanding the concept of Bushido of finding life (Sei 生) in the death (Shi 殺), which implies accepting that once born one day you will inevitably die (the "Kesshi no Kakuro" 決死の覚悟, a willingness to face death). Once you close your eyes, you should not think about anything, and do not sink into yourself, but should rather be "connected". To use our sixth sense is therefore very important to relax and to not think "Mushin" 無心.

The "Mind that is something" is equal to the confused mind and is designed literally as the "Mind that exists". It is the mind that directs your thoughts in one direction, regardless of the person to whom it is addressed. When the mind is a source of thought, there are prejudices and discrimination.
The "No Mind" (Mushin 無心) is equal to the right-minded. Does not freeze and is not fixed in one spot. It is called "No mind" when there are no thoughts and discriminations and the mind roams free in the body, completely permeating the Self. The "No mind" is not in any place . The mind stops and stays in one place does not act freely. The mind is also something that would not work if you were to bind to a single situation. When a thought occupies the mind, even if you hear the words spoken, you are not really able to understand them. This happens because the mind is at rest with the thought that occupies it. What is in the mind is thinking. If you are able to remove it, the mind will become "no mind", if necessary, and will always act in accordance with its function .

    An ancient poem reads:

> Think : I do not think
> This is already something in his own thoughts.
> Simply, do not think
> What you should not think .

No one should expect something special, because this will ensure that the mind is fixed, and so you will not be able to feel the Sakki and avoid the Fukuro Shinai, and it should be understood that the sensation varies from person to person. Another very important thing is to know how to roll well, so that once perceived the intention, one can roll away in a natural way , in fact this aspect is taken into consideration at the time of the examination .
This exam for us practitioners of Bujinkan is very important, because this initiation through the sixth sense allows the understanding of Myojutsu 妙術 (mysterious art), leading to Myougi 妙技 (mysterious techniques).
"If you think that you understand, in fact you have not got it, if you think you do not understand it, then you have got it".

Shinbu Fusatsu
"The divine Budo is not for killing", the real Budo is to beat the opponent without killing him.

Glossary

Ashiko 足甲: claws for feet of Togakure Ryu

Atemi 当て身: blow to a vital point of a person's body

Atemi no tanren 当身の鍛錬: conditioning techniques of the body weapons

Banpenfugyo 万変不驚: 10,000 changes no surprise

Bansenshukai 萬川集海: book of the XVII century history and techniques of Iga and Koga Shinobi

Bo 棒: stick (rokushakubo 六尺棒 six feet tall stick)

Budo 武道: matial arts

Bokken – Bokuto 木剣: wooden sword

Budoka 武道家: martial artist

Bufu-ikkan 武風一貫: the martial way as a rule, each day of your life, literally, "living through martial wind"

Bujinkan 武神館: residence of the god of war

Buyu 武友: martial artist friend

Daisho 大小: large and small; matched pair of long and short swords (symbol of the samurai caste)

Fudoshin 不動心: imperturbable spirit (or immutable)

Ganbatte 頑張って: do your best; go for it; hold on; keep at it

Gokui 極意: deepest level (of an art, skill, etc.); secret teachings; mysteries; innermost secrets

Gorin 五輪: five rings

Goshinjutsu 護身術: art of self-defense; art of self-defence

Gotonpo 五遁法: methods of escape of the five elements

Gyaku 逆: reverse; opposite; joint-lock

Hanbo 半棒: short cane staff

Happobiken 八法秘剣: eight methods of secret sword

Henka 変化: change; variation; alteration; mutation; transition; transformation

Hidari 左: left

Hoko no jutsu 歩行の術: furtively walk techniques

Jutsu 術: art; technique

Kaiten 回転: roll; rotation; revolution

Kakushi Buki 隠し武器: concealed weapons

Kanji 漢字: Chinese characters

Kankaku 感覚: sense; sensation; feeling; intuition

Kata 型: model; type; pattern; standard form of a movement

Katana 刀: (single-edged) japanese sword

Kihon Waza 基本技: basic techniques

Kyojitsu 虚実: truth and falsehood, feint

Migi 右: right

Nagashi 流し: flow

Nage 投げ: to throw; to cast away

Rei 礼: thanks; gratitude; manners; etiquette; bow; reward; gift; ceremony; ritual

Ryu 流: fashion; way; style; manner; school

Sakkijutsu 殺気術: techniques to perceive the murderous intent

Sennin 仙人: immortal mountain wizard (in Taoism); mountain man

Senpai 先輩: senior (at work or school); superior; elder

Sensei 先生: teacher; master

Shingitai Ichi Jo 心技体一情: the heart, the technique and the body acting as one

Shugendo 修験道: Japanese mountain asceticism-shamanism incorporating Shinto and Buddhist concepts

Shuko 手甲: claws for hands of Togakure Ryu

Shihan 師範: Title of "Master" is a Japanese Honorific Title, Expert

Soke 宗家: the head family. In the realm of Japanese traditional arts, it is used synonymously with the term iemoto. Thus, it is often used to indicate "headmaster"

Taisabaki 体捌き: body movement

Tantou 短刀: short sword; dagger

Tengu 天狗: long-nosed goblin. They lived in the mountains considered leading experts in martial arts

Japanese numbers

Ichi 一 : one

Ni 二 : two

San 三 : three

Shi (Yon) 四 : four

Go 五 : five

Roku 六 : six

Shichi (Nana) 七 : seven

Hachi 八 : eight

Ku (Kyu) 九 : nine

Ju 十 : ten

Ju ichi 十一 : eleven

Ju ni 十二 : twelve

Ju ku 十九 : nineteen

Ni ju 二十 : twenty

San ju 三十 : thirty

Shi ju 四十 : fourty

Go ju 五十 : fifty

Hyaku 百 : hundred

Sen 千 : thousand

Ban 万 : ten thousand

The author:

The Shihan 師範 Luca Lanaro (Shihan means Title of "Master" is a Japanese Honorific Title) he got the degree of Jugodan (15th Dan) Kugyo Happobiken 十五段 空行八法秘剣, is regularly registered at Shidoshikai (internationally accredited instructors of Bujinkan), and teaches in Genoa from 1999, every year he goes to Japan to study directly with Soke Masaaki Hatsumi, also he gives seminars in Italy and abroad. He was awarded by Soke Masaaki Hatsumi with martial name (Bugou 武号) Isamu Koma 勇駒 which can be translated as "brave horse" (Koma 駒 is the ideogram for chess horse Japanese Shogi, which is a very important piece, while Isamu 勇 means; brave, courageous and heroic).

Website: http://bujin.altervista.org/index.php
Facebook: Bujinkan Dojo Genova
Youtube: Bujinkan Dojo Genova
Email: infobujinkan@gmail.com